To my dear
+ neighbour
All the best for 2...
Patricia
Jan 26/12

SMART MOUTH!
Helping you Communicate

SMART MOUTH!
Helping you Communicate

Patrice M. McKenzie, M.S.Ed., C.N.H.P.

iUniverse, Inc.
Bloomington

Smart Mouth
Helping You Communicate

Copyright © 2011 by Patrice M. McKenzie

All rights reserved. No part of this book may be used or reproduced by
any means, graphic, electronic, or mechanical, including photocopying,
recording, taping or by any information storage retrieval system
without the written permission of the publisher except in the case
of brief quotations embodied in critical articles and reviews.

Design by Sarah Vincett, BigRedDesign, Toronto, Canada
Illustrations by Duncan Keeley, Toronto, Canada

iUniverse books may be ordered through booksellers or by contacting:

iUniverse
1663 Liberty Drive
Bloomington, IN 47403
www.iuniverse.com
1-800-Authors (1-800-288-4677)

Because of the dynamic nature of the Internet, any web addresses or links contained in
this book may have changed since publication and may no longer be valid. The views
expressed in this work are solely those of the author and do not necessarily reflect the
views of the publisher, and the publisher hereby disclaims any responsibility for them.

Any people depicted in stock imagery provided by Thinkstock are models,
and such images are being used for illustrative purposes only.

Certain stock imagery © Thinkstock.

ISBN: 978-1-4620-3015-6 (sc)
ISBN: 978-1-4620-3016-3 (e)

Library of Congress Control Number: 2011909947

Printed in the United States of America

iUniverse rev. date: 9/12/2011

Dedication

To my aunt Hellen who demonstrated anything is possible through courage and mindfulness, and to my children, Tristan, Melissa and Andrew who are a testament to everything good, loving, and sound. You are the architects of my backbone.

Contents

Chapter 1	What Is Effective Communication?	1
Chapter 2	Barriers to Effective Communication	10
Chapter 3	Why Positive Self-Esteem Is Essential to Effective Communication	19
Chapter 4	Useful Theories to Understand	35
Chapter 5	The Who and Why of Communication	57
Chapter 6	The What and Where of Communication	74
Chapter 7	The When of Communication	83
Chapter 8	Pattern Interrupt	88
Chapter 9	Be Proactive, Not Reactive	95
Chapter 10	Listen, Listen, Listen	108
Chapter 11	Body Language	116
Chapter 12	The Authentic Self	126
Chapter 13	Speak My Language Too	134
Chapter 14	Let Go, Look for the Win-Win—You Don't Have to Prove You're an Expert	141
Chapter 15	Respect Yourself, Validate Others	148
Chapter 16	The Learning Curve	162
Chapter 17	Intuition	174
Chapter 18	Determining If You Have a Disagreement	182
Chapter 19	Tools for Differing Opinions and Disagreements	189
Chapter 20	Communicating with Difficult People	196
Chapter 21	Forgiveness	202
Chapter 22	You Will Achieve What You Believe or Fake It Till You Make It!	213

Foreword

It is an honour to have the opportunity to write this foreword for a number of reasons. The author is known to me from a number of perspectives. First, as my graduate student in a master's of counselling program, then as a professional colleague, and finally one who has become a close family friend. It is personally rewarding to have been able to observe and be part of her professional development. Twenty-three years ago, as a student in my interpersonal communications course and various other courses within the graduate counselling program, I sensed her potential for making significant contributions to the professional field. Since then she has, through clinical practice and work experiences, been able to refine and expand her knowledge, enabling her to author, in my opinion, an outstanding book.

I feel comfortable writing this foreword based on my academic credentials at the bachelor's and master's levels while, for a decade, teaching and counselling secondary students. After obtaining my doctoral degree, I solidified my career as a university professor and counselor educator for the next thirty-three years, some of which were spent as department of education chairperson. All these experiences confirmed my belief success is predicated by one's ability to communicate clearly and directly.

The overriding strength of this handy personal guide is its efficacy. The material is applicable to a variety of uses by professionals, students at various academic levels, practitioners, and the public at large.

After forty years of having read numerous books and journal articles on the topic of communication, I look for a new work to inspire, teach, inform, and make useable valid material contained therein. This book provides a practical hands-on format, which allows the reader to identify with the material, simplifies complex theories and processes of communication, and makes them easily understood and usable. As a result, the reader will be able to not only learn from the book but also experience personal growth through introspection and application. The charts, case study examples, and the author's personal disclosures lead the reader to easily understand concepts and strategies of communication, which, when used, will result in more rewarding interpersonal relationships. Additionally, the book is nonthreatening and demystifies the science and art of effective communication. Finally, as a personal guide, the book delivers exactly what it should. It is short, concise, to the point, and can be easily read and internalized.

Individuals pursuing self-examination and personal growth in their relationships, whether they are work, social, family, intimate, or school related, will find this book helpful in getting in touch with themselves. Persons who are presently troubled or experiencing conflicts in their life will find the book instructional in learning coping skills, how to overcome barriers, and how to develop supportive relationships. Students pursuing a career in the psychosocial sciences will likewise find the book provides a solid grounding in the basics of communications.

Having participated in the field-testing of this book through my classes with future social workers, psychologists, teachers, counselors (school, agency, mental health, etcetera), professional counselors in the field, and through clients in the author's private practice, feedback established the approaches and techniques in the book are easily understood, learned, and applied. It was also noted the case studies presented in the book facilitated an opportunity for students to review and consolidate theory, learned knowledge, and skills. Actual clients have said the book validates the therapeutic process.

In conclusion, my goal in endorsing this book is to encourage readers to continue their journey of personal growth and development by using the book as a vehicle to further strengthen or change elements within their own personal communication.

Salvatore Pappalardo, Ed.D.
Professor of Counselor Education (retired)
Adjunct Professor of Counselor Education (present)
Niagara University, NY

Preface

In my counselling experience, the overriding issue blocking interpersonal, emotional and psychological health is an inability to communicate well. This book had its origins as a communications skills training component that I developed and began integrating into the treatment process over two decades ago and which over the intervening period I have delivered at dozens of workshops and seminars.

Audiences enthusiastically embraced these presentations, which confirmed my belief that the public needs, and wants, more information on how to achieve and sustain successful interpersonal communications; hence, this book which draws upon the workshops and seminars, using, as examples, actual cases from my private practice (with the names of clients changed). The book is rooted in the struggles and experiences, failures and successes, of real people like you and me.

The book, which has been extensively field-tested, covers the basic skills one needs to communicate well. It describes what effective communication is: the who, what, why, when, and where of communication; challenges to communication; the art of listening; maintaining and respecting your authentic self; validating others; handling disagreements and difficult people; and how to forgive. Most importantly, it is designed so that readers can implement the concepts simply and easily -- and achieve real, positive results.

Acknowledgments

Over three decades I have been given the opportunity and privilege to work with hundreds of individuals, couples, and families. Their personal stories and journeys encouraged me to stretch my skills and build my competence; without them, this book would not have been possible.

I would also like to thank my professors, advisors, and clinical supervisors over the years as well as colleagues whose guidance, insight, and support have proven invaluable. A special thanks to Dr. Salvatore Pappalardo and Dr. Paul Vermette of Niagara University for facilitating the publishing process.

Members of the Niagara and Orleans Counseling Association and the Western New York Suburban Counselors Consortium took the time to read and edit the manuscript. Your professional advice and encouragement was greatly appreciated.

Introduction

Learning how to communicate well can be long and frustrating which is why I have written this personal guide.

Whether it is a conflict between partners, parents and children, employers and employees, teachers and students, etc., the underlying cause is almost always miscommunication. How many times have you heard "she/he just doesn't listen to me," "if you would only try to understand what I am saying," "nobody seems to understand me," "there you go again," "why do you always misinterpret what I'm saying?" "why don't you try listening to me for a change?" "no, that wasn't what I said," "why don't you talk to me anymore?" and so on?

Although people are naturally social, I do not believe we are born with the innate ability to communicate clearly and directly. Communicating well takes time and patience. It is a process of using skills and techniques to enhance and promote a clear and positive exchange. It is the act of investing in yourself and another to ensure what you say is accurately delivered and understood. It also entails listening attentively to catch the true meaning (thoughts and feelings) of what is being said to you and checking in with the speaker to make sure your understanding is accurate.

This book will help you understand some basic concepts about the art of communication; provide some user-friendly, practical tools, and techniques which can be easily put to use; and give some case examples to demonstrate the ease with which these simple tools can be applied. Time and time again clients have shown me they are capable of creating more fulfilling and rewarding lives based on how they choose to communicate. The strategies I recommend have been suitably tested, work well, and are endorsed by over two decades' worth of clients.

The concepts and principles found in this book are based on theory, my counselling practice, and from personal experience - both good and bad. I, too, have walked a path of discovery through childhood, adulthood (including divorce), and parenthood and continue a journey of lifelong learning. Now is a good time for you to begin to use your past experiences as your teacher and not your judge and open yourself to learn new ways of thinking and behaving with a goal to becoming a better communicator.

Chapter One
What Is Effective Communication?

Effective communication is the ability to send your message in a clear, direct and understandable way. It is twofold, as the act of communicating may result in receiving a response. It is then up to you to listen intently, seek clarification if necessary to ensure your understanding is accurate, and then validate the message you have received. Sounds easy; in fact, it sounds too easy.

🔍 The Case of the CEO and Manager

On a late Friday afternoon, the CEO of a large corporation met his manager of operations in the elevator. He apologized to the manager but asked him to put some figures together on the year's last quarter in preparation for an impromptu meeting he was having with one of their international clients first thing Monday morning. With barely a smile, the manager quickly sped to his office, met with his staff, and informed them they were required to work late in order to create the appropriate spreadsheets, forecasts, etc. The manager and staff worked with diligence as the sun dropped behind their building but were proud to have produced a comprehensive binder of information.

Chapter One | What is Effective Communication?

At eight o'clock Monday morning, the manager, filled with confidence and content with the work done by him and his staff, presented the CEO with the binder. The CEO was shocked and replied, "I didn't want this, how will I ever get through all this information by the time my client arrives in an hour? Whatever possessed you to produce this?" The manager was horrified.

What happened in the elevator exchange between the CEO and the manager? How did their communication go so terribly wrong? Who was in error? If you said "both were in error," you are correct. Let's take a closer look. To begin, the CEO failed to give the manager all the information the manager needed to do the work required. He did not tell him who the client was, the focus of the meeting, the type of information needed, the length of the report, or how he wanted the information presented. The manager, on the other hand, *assumed* he knew what the CEO wanted and didn't ask for clarification. The manager went forward with a preconceived concept or idea without testing his idea against the CEO's expectations. In fact, all the CEO wanted was a two- or three- page executive summary or briefing note on the company's profit and loss statement for the last quarter.

Asking questions for the purpose of clarification is important. There is no such thing as a silly question; there are only silly answers and silly assumptions.

The Case of Shelly (Mother) and Dawn (Daughter)

I was seeing a mother and her eighteen-year-old daughter for counselling. The mother complained of not being respected, being used, suffering verbal abuse from her daughter, and being lied to. The daughter claimed her mother was too controlling, never minded her own business, and never listened to her point of view. They told me about the following incident.

The daughter approached her mom to ask if she could use the car the following Saturday evening. The mom said okay. That was the end of their communication.

When Saturday came along and the clock struck 8:00 PM, the daughter was furious there was no car or mother to be found. A half hour later, Mom arrived home after having spent a wonderful dinner with friends even though she cut her evening short to get the car home for Dawn. A heated argument between mom and daughter ensued, ruining everyone's evening and reinforcing both the mother's belief of suffering verbal abuse and being used and the daughter's belief of not being heard. Upon further clarification, however, we were able to discover the following: the daughter had waited until just prior to Mom retiring to bed to ask for permission to use the car. Mom was tired and not really up to a lot of conversation. Dawn never did say what time she needed the car. Mom didn't ask the daughter about a time because she *assumed*, based on previous experience, the daughter would not be leaving the house until around 9:00 PM.

A few important lessons can be learned here. Timing is everything. I firmly believe you can tell anyone anything in five minutes or less as long as you pick your timing carefully. Meaningful exchanges rarely happen when people are tired, upset, ill, or angry. Again, give the person enough information to ensure they are adequately informed. Conversely, if you have not been given enough information, ask questions. Never *assume* anything; you are usually wrong. Always enter into a dialogue with the intention of fair play, openness, and honesty and believe you will receive the same in return. Otherwise, you may feed into your own negative belief system about another person and fuel your own insecurities.

So then, why is it so easy to talk to a best friend? Best friends are not out to win, control, outdo, judge, or hurt you. They have taken the necessary time to understand how you think. They have presented you with their vulnerabilities and have accepted the authentic you. Best friends are not afraid to cry or laugh in front of you, will tell you when you are angering them because they don't fear the loss of your friendship, and will trust you as much as they trust themselves. People become best friends not only because they share common interests, but also because they have learned the art of communicating well together. They have also learned to pick up on each other's body language and subtle nuances. Best friends demonstrate *responsibility* and the *ability* to *respond*, and most of all, best friends demonstrate *active listening skills*.

Active listening employs a few simple techniques. To begin, the active listener looks directly at and leans slightly toward the communicator. Their body posture is relaxed and open as if to say, "I am very interested in what you have to say; you are important to me." The active listener will ask open-ended questions, which are questions that invite additional comment from the communicator, for example, "That sounds very exciting; what happened next?" or "What did you think about that?" Additionally, the active listener will engage in *paraphrasing*. Paraphrasing is the ability to interpret what someone has just said to you by saying it back to the speaker for their approval. This technique has a dual function. It sends a message to the communicator that you have been listening to what they have been saying; in other words, you have been *attending* to them. Attending to the communicator sends a message of positive regard, respect, and genuine interest. Paraphrasing also gives the listener an opportunity to seek clarification of the facts and confirm or get clarification to ensure what the listener has heard is accurate. The following is an example:

> COMMUNICATOR. As I was leaving school yesterday, the principal stopped me and began asking me a lot of questions about the colleges I was thinking of applying to next year. She not only asked me about that but also started asking me about my grade point average, how I felt about my marks, and if there was anything I could be doing to improve my grades.

> LISTENER. The principal was making a lot of inquiries about your chances of being successful in getting into college next year.

In this simple exchange, the communicator shared vital information with the listener. The listener demonstrated he valued what the communicator was saying and he wanted to be sure he was interpreting the communicator accurately. Let's take this exchange and the skill of paraphrasing one step further.

> COMMUNICATOR. Yes, I felt the principal was trying to tell me my grades weren't good enough. It made me quite uncomfortable.

> LISTENER. Tell me what you think about your grades and what colleges you might be applying to.

As you can see from the above example, the listener was able to assist the communicator to continue with his thoughts and verbalize them. The listener encouraged the communication by joining with the communicator and supporting the dialogue.

Here is another example of paraphrasing:

COMMUNICATOR (Husband). I am calling the staff together today to discuss a new performance-review process the company is implementing. I don't think the staff is going to like it.

LISTENER (Wife). You think the staff is going to have a difficult time with the new process?

COMMUNICATOR (Husband). No, I don't think they'll have difficulty with the new process once they understand it; I just don't think they will like the idea of having their performance reviewed.

By paraphrasing what the wife thought she heard her husband say, she gave the communicator an opportunity to clarify the message and restate it.

Let's review some facts about effective communication. Communication is the verbal and nonverbal exchange of one's thoughts and feelings between two or more people. To communicate effectively, all parties must *attend* to each other and demonstrate positive regard and genuine intent. Effective communicators are not motivated by a need to control, win, outdo, or judge but think of themselves as an equal, responsible partner joined in an exchange. They employ techniques which will encourage a positive, clear, and continuous dialogue.

Effective communication is made up of two parts: the person who is speaking and the person who is listening. Effective communicators ensure their ideas are articulated clearly and directly, they give the listener adequate information, and they do not put the listener into a position of having to *assume* what is being said. They respect the listener by pausing to give the listener time to digest the information, and they do not overburden the listener with too much information. They know where and when not to engage in a communication, and they use understandable language.

Let's go back to the earlier mother-daughter scenario where the daughter requested the use of the car the following Saturday evening. After having been asked for the use of the car, the mother had two response options. The first response could have been, "I don't think there will be a problem, but it's very late, and I'm too tired to think right now. I'd like to talk with you about our mutual plans for Saturday night tomorrow morning over breakfast." This response is telling the daughter (a) I have heard your request (validation),

(b) inasmuch as I am too tired to address the issue right now, I would like to speak with you tomorrow (joining), (c) I would like to talk to you tomorrow at a specific time, i.e., breakfast (clarity), and (d) I may have plans as well for Saturday night (clarity).

The second response the mother could have given is, "Yes, I think we can work together on this. I am planning to have dinner with my friends Saturday night, but I can plan on being home by nine. Would that work for you?" This response tells the daughter (a) I have heard your request (validation), (b) I also have plans for Saturday evening (clarity), but (c) I invite you to work with me to come up with a mutually agreeable time (joining).

Listeners, on the other hand, have the job of being attentive, open, and receptive; of inviting continued dialogue by asking open-ended questions; and of paraphrasing what the communicator has said. Their body language is open and inviting, and they focus all their attention onto the communicator to invite continued dialogue. They never presume to think they know what the communicator is saying without seeking clarification. They send the message, "I value you, and I think what you are saying is important."

Take every opportunity to practice being a better communicator and don't be discouraged if it doesn't always work out the way you thought it might. Remember, you are only one half of the communications process, and you can only be responsible for your half. It takes work and courage to communicate well. Practice, practice, practice!

👉 Points to Remember From Chapter One

- Effective communication is the ability to listen attentively, seek clarification, and respond appropriately.

- Never *assume* you understand what someone is thinking or feeling. You will usually be wrong.

- Timing is important. Meaningful exchanges rarely happen when you are tired, upset, ill, angry, or in a hurry.

- Communication is blocked when you try to win, control, outdo, judge, or hurt someone else.

- Effective communication means acting *responsibly*, i.e., demonstrating the *ability* to listen intently and *respond*.

- Active listening means demonstrating attentive body language, asking open-ended questions, and paraphrasing what the communicator has said.

- A good communicator will demonstrate positive regard and genuine intent.

- An effective communicator articulates clearly and uses understandable language.

Chapter One | What is Effective Communication?

What Have I Learned From This Chapter That Applies to Me?

What Will I Begin To Do Differently?

Chapter Two
Barriers to Effective Communication

Now that we know what effective communication is, let's take a look at some of the barriers. Barriers result when people sabotage the communications process. I am sure you can remember a time when a conversation resulted in confusion or a misunderstanding.

🔍 The Case of Don and Marge

Don and Marge had been married for nine years when they came for counselling. They had been relatively happy for the first half of their marriage but felt their relationship had deteriorated over the past five or so years. They were very clear about their feelings of aloneness and irritation toward each other. A few interesting details emerged from the initial consultation.

When the couple entered the office, Don and Marge sat at opposite ends of the sofa across from me. Don rested his arm on the upper left back of the sofa with the tips of his fingers a few inches from Marge's right shoulder. His outstretched legs were crossed at the ankle. Marge, on the other hand, sat on the right side of the sofa, her hands folded on her lap, legs crossed at the knees, facing away from Don.

The sculpting of Don and Marge's seating arrangement gives us a few clues to their relationship. Don and Marge do not feel comfortable sitting physically close. Don's body language is open and relaxed, and he appears to be reaching toward Marge. Marge's body language, however, is very closed. Her hands are folded and close to her body, and her legs are crossed in front of her almost as though to protect herself. She did not feel comfortable facing Don.

As Don began to tell his story, a few things emerged. Don always referred to Marge as "she." During parts of his conversation, his voice would lift to a booming crescendo. During these times, his body would lift from the sofa, enlarging his already-large frame as he waved his arms about him. He continued to point out all the things "she" should be doing to improve the marriage and was able to provide "her" with examples of what he meant by improvement. When Marge did not respond to him, he began to ask her an excessive number of questions, most of which began with the word *why*. For example, "Why can't you just stay at the

table after we have finished dinner and visit with me? Why do you always have to jump up and start the dishes?" Before concluding his story, he threw in a derogatory comment about Marge's regular Tuesday-night tennis game.

During Don's presentation, Marge's shoulders slumped forward, she began wringing her hands, and she stared off to a small spot on the ceiling. She attempted to hide her tears from Don's vision as the blue of her eyes turned to grey.

Let's look at how Don sabotaged any attempt to engage in a positive communication with Marge. In chapter one, we talked about the importance of demonstrating positive regard and genuine intent; in other words, the requirement to join with another as a partner each having responsibility for the success of the outcome. We talked about being non-judgmental and not harbouring ulterior motives such as the need to win, control, or outdo the other.

Don began blocking the communication by constantly referring to his wife as "she." The word *she* is a pronoun, which may refer to a female person. *She* may also refer to a boat, a car, a country, your pet kitten, or any number of other things. The word *wife*, on the other hand, is a noun and refers specifically to a married woman. In this case, the woman married to Don. Don could have also used Marge's name when referring to his wife. Had he chosen either of these options, Don would have been demonstrating his respect and positive regard toward Marge.

Don then began to raise his voice to an almost-frightening pitch. In addition to his booming voice, Don used his body to look even larger as he raised himself off the sofa while at the same time waving his arms about. Both of these behaviours may be labeled intimidation. The intent of intimidation is usually to seek control, affirm one's position of authority, and instill fear in others.

Don also had a lot of advice to give Marge about how she could improve their relationship. Unwanted advice often leaves the listener feeling defensive and exasperated, which leads to rejection. Advice giving also leaves the listener with a feeling of inadequacy as though they were a child and unable to function on their own. When a person engages in a great deal of advice giving, it can be termed *lecturing*. Lecturing sends a clear message to the listener that the communicator is the expert. Heaven forbid if the listener should not take their advice. This would only reinforce to the communicator how stupid the listener is and potentially lead to an angered communicator if their advice was not followed. Lecturing typically leads to the listener just *turning off* and staring at a small spot on the ceiling as in Marge's case.

To try and bring Marge's attention back to him, Don began to ask her a lot of questions, thus attempting to force a response and reinforce his power over her. He became the interrogator and pushed Marge further into a defensive mode. "Why" questions are even more damaging because they attempt to force the listener into a position of having to justify or defend their thoughts, actions, and feelings.

When Don failed to hook Marge into his communication, he tried inflicting one final blow by making a derogatory comment about her regular Tuesday-night tennis game, which was already a sore spot between them. In other words, Don tried to **push her button**.

Don also failed to use any *I* words during his presentation, thus denying any personal responsibility in the relationship.

After examining Don's behaviour, it is not surprising Marge's body language spoke to her need for protection resulting in her *shutting down*.

Another breakdown in communication exists when the listener interrupts and does not allow the communicator to complete his or her sentence or thought. As you see, *butting in* sends a very complex message to the communicator. It says, (a) "I don't think what you are saying is important, so you needn't bother finishing your statement," (b) "I think what you are saying is wrong," (c) "I think what your saying is stupid," (d) "I think you need to listen to me because I can enlighten you," (e) "I am more important than you are," (f) "I want to be the centre of attention," (g) I really don't think much of you, so it's okay for me to act rudely toward you," and so on.

The Case of Mark (Son) and Ben (Father)

MARK. Sometimes I have difficulty concentrating at school. I begin to daydream and—

BEN, *butting in*. You daydream because you are girl crazy, and you can't keep your mind on what's important.

MARK. That's not true, Dad; I'm not girl crazy, and I do try to follow what's going on in class but—

BEN, *butting in*. But nothing, and don't give me that. You just don't care about school.

MARK. That's not fair. If you'd only give me a chance to explain, you would understand—

BEN, *butting in*. I'm sick of trying to understand you. You're just full of excuses. Why should I believe you anyway?

After reading this exchange, I don't think anyone would want to be in Mark's shoes. In this very short exchange, Ben interrupted his son each time Mark spoke. In addition to the constant interruptions, Ben also sent all the negative messages mentioned above, namely, "I am in charge," "you aren't important," and "you don't know what you are talking about."

Chapter Two | Barriers to Effective Communication

The lesson, therefore, is to listen fully until the communicator has completed what it is they have to say, paraphrase if appropriate, and respond with positive regard and respect.

Let's repeat the Ben and Mark scenario by using what we learned in chapter 1.

> MARK. Sometimes I have difficulty concentrating at school. I begin to daydream, and the next thing I know I am falling asleep. It really bothers me.
>
> BEN. Yes, I can understand how upsetting that would be. What are your thoughts about why it is happening?
>
> MARK. I don't know. Did this ever happen to you in school?
>
> BEN. I have had this happen. Sometimes I was just overly tired. Other times my mind wandered off to thoughts about my girlfriend or an upcoming ball game. And sometimes, class just bored me. However, we pay dearly for falling asleep in class, and we all have to pay the consequences.
>
> MARK. I'm going to have to check myself closely the next time my mind starts to wander.
>
> BEN. I know getting into college is a priority for you and you will do everything possible to keep your grades up. I'm glad you told me about this. Let me know if there is anything I can do.

What a contrast between this interaction and the earlier dialogue between Mark and Ben. The father gave his son the opportunity to share his thoughts and empathized with the son's concern. Ben, at his son's request, was also able to offer a few suggestions as to why Mark may be falling asleep. Ben was non-judgmental and showed respect and positive regard for Mark by believing in his ability to handle the situation while at the same time leaving the door open for a follow-up discussion.

Intellectualizing and "one-ups-man-ship" are another two threats to effective communication. I recently met an acquaintance on the elevator and asked how her weekend was. She responded with so many run-on sentences comprised of so many multiple-syllable words I had difficulty understanding what she was saying. I had no idea the description of one's weekend could be so complex and be expressed with such intellectual superiority. I believe *pompous* would be a good word to describe my acquaintance's behaviour. I'm glad I didn't ask about her whole week.

Some simple rules to keep in mind to ensure communication will not break down are as follows: face the person you are interacting with and look into their eyes, be sure your body language and voice are friendly and relaxed, refer to the person by his/her name, let the person finish his/her thought before responding, employ paraphrasing if it is appropriate, don't ask questions that will make the person feel uncomfortable and out of control, don't lecture, don't butt in or act superior, and most of all, end your communication on a positive note.

Chapter Two | Barriers to Effective Communication

👉 Points to Remember From Chapter Two

Barriers to communication include the following:

- Failing to show respect and positive regard

- Sabotaging the conversation

- Failing to be clear

- If you are the listener, failing to ensure what you heard was accurate

- Failing to be empathic if necessary

- Advice giving

- Intimidation tactics like raising your voice or waving your arms around

- Questioning or interrogating the communicator

- Inappropriate advice giving

- Butting in

- Intellectualizing

- Poor body language, especially not looking directly at the person with whom you are speaking

What Will I Begin To Do Differently?

Chapter Two | Barriers to Effective Communication

What Will I Begin To Do Differently?

Chapter Three
Why Positive Self-Esteem Is Essential to Effective Communication

I was traveling on the subway this morning and saw an inspired advertisement. It was a picture of a bird's egg snuggled in a small nest. An infant, instead of a bird, was breaking out of the shell. All that peeked out was a miniature smiling cherubic head. The caption under the picture read, "Will a child stay in an emotional shell or emerge sunny-side up? The first five years stay the rest of their lives." This strong message speaks to us about our feelings of self-worth, self-love, self-respect, and self-esteem. It speaks to the powerful impact our parents, other care givers, and those around us had and have in shaping our self-esteem. It also speaks to the responsibility we have to ensure our young people emerge with abundant feelings of self-worth.

Self-esteem can be defined as how much value you place on yourself or what you think of yourself, measured against what you think you should be, or how much you approve or disapprove of yourself measured against your idealized self. People with high self-esteem feel good about themselves and like being in their own company. Even when some things go wrong in their lives, they work to change the conditions as opposed to blaming themselves and becoming the victim. They have mastered the art of committing themselves to everything they do in the fullest possible way. They know they are important.

Rarely anyone would score 100 percent on a self-esteem score because no one has been raised by perfect people in a perfect world. However, it is safe to say we should be aiming for a *general* sense of positive self-worth.

Abraham Maslow, a noted psychologist, theorized the average American satisfies perhaps 90 percent of their physical needs (food, water, sleep, oxygen), 70 percent of their safety needs (shelter, stable environment), 50 percent of love needs (support and affection from others), 40 percent of esteem needs (self-respect), and 10 percent of the need for self-actualization (your need to fulfill your potential in life). In order to have a general sense of positive self-worth, it is imperative we are able to recognize and work to satisfy each of these needs.

Self-esteem affects everything we do, including the way we take care of ourselves and those we love, the way we do our jobs, and how we communicate to express our creativity, uniqueness, and individuality to others. It impacts our life choices, our success, and our ultimate happiness.

Its development began at a deep subconscious level, so deep it's confusing to understand. It is comprised of thousands of messages and experiences our mind has filed away, now long forgotten. Many of these messages happened when we were infants and toddlers, before we could speak and put words to events to understand them. Needless to say, many understandings and beliefs formulated at this time, many of which we continue to think of as *core beliefs*, are really erroneous. Nonetheless, this compilation of messages, thoughts, and experiences manifests itself in defining what we think about ourselves today.

People with poor self-esteem practice self-imposed limiting behaviours. They rarely take risks because of fear of failure, they do not fare well socially because their belief system tells them they are not lovable, they are their own best critic judging rather than praising their thoughts and behaviours and lack self-respect because they think they just aren't good enough. People like this rely on others to define who they are and fall easy victims to their environment. They thrive on a self-fulfilling prophecy of negative attitudes and behaviours and attract people who will mirror these negative concepts. Some will purposely put themselves into a negative situation just to reinforce their own feelings of failure. They believe negative attention is better than no attention at all.

Negative self-esteem results in emotional and psychological asphyxiation, where one cuts off or blocks important parts of their innermost being out of fear of being hurt. As one alters their inner constructs, new unhealthy and self-defeating behaviours emerge, which soon become a normal way of functioning. These self-defeating behaviours are rewarded by failures, thus reinforcing these dysfunctional patterns and so on and so on. What is even more frightening, these dysfunctional patterns can be passed on from generation to generation until someone breaks the cycle.

Many clients know their actions are self-defeating but don't understand how they got there or why they stay there. The "how they got there" is easier to explain than the "why they stay there." To begin, let's go back to the small infant sitting inside the bird's egg. The child is an expression of untouched perfection, trusting in his or her parents and the world to care for and protect him or her always. In many cases, this is exactly what parents and the extended family do. However, there are situations where children are not provided with the comfort, care, protection, and positive environment an evolving child requires resulting in poor self-esteem. Negative self-worth may also result from the conditions in which a child is raised. Poverty, war, and illness are not the best prescription for one's long-term mental health. These are only a few examples of why one grows into adulthood under a cloak of negative self-worth.

More importantly, people should believe the world at large is a good and safe place in which to grow, be aware of their needs and how to satisfy them. So often people are not even aware of what they need because they have experienced a history of deprivation. For example, I know I need financial security and a comfortable home. I need to know my children and grandchildren feel loved by me and I am loved by them. I need to have a circle of close friends. I need to be listened to and shown respect. I need to succeed at work and I need to give something back to my community.

Chapter Three | Why Positive Self-Esteem Is Essential to Effective Communication

I'm sure I could come up with a much longer list of needs, but by now you probably understand where I am coming from. I believe if people spent more time understanding what their needs were and developing goals and corresponding action plans to achieve their goals, we would live in a much happier world. Energy can be better spent building self-esteem than exhausting it on blaming others, nay saying and justifying one's negative actions.

The more difficult question to answer is why people choose to stay in a negative position. I describe this phenomenon to clients as living in one's *comfort zone*. Try to imagine a five- inch band stretched in front of you. Everything that goes on inside the band is so-called normal, comfortable, and predictable even if what goes on in there is unhealthy, perhaps even insane. People stay in their comfort zones and rarely jump up and out of it or dive below it because that would mean leaving what is comfortable and moving into a world of the unknown. Oftentimes people do not want to leave their comfort zones because they believe they don't belong there or they are undeserving. The comfort zone is very rewarding because as long as one stays there, you know you have the capacity to handle it. We have spent years perfecting the behaviours that keep us in the comfort zone and, moreover, have learned to relate to everyone around us based on where we position ourselves within it.

🔍 The Case of Charles and Katy

Charles and Katy had been married for almost ten years. Katy encouraged Charles to join her in marriage counselling with a goal of freeing herself from a history of Charles's degrading verbal abuse, which, among other things, included name-calling and blaming. This negative behaviour had been going on since their early years but increasingly became worse as time passed. Katy chose not to deal with his aggressive language any longer but was having difficulty persuading Charles to change, as he did not believe he was doing anything wrong.

Charles worked in the auto industry on the assembly line. He enjoyed working overtime, which inflated his already very lucrative salary. He and Katy lived comfortably, were debt-free, and enjoyed regular annual vacations. They had no children.

Katy worked as an assistant manager in a woman's clothing store. She enjoyed her work. It gave her an opportunity to interact with the public, which she enjoyed. She also benefited by being able to wear the latest line of fashion designs compliments of her company. She enjoyed dressing up. It made her feel good about herself.

Charles grew up in a lower-income neighborhood. His father was a labourer. His mother left Charles and his four siblings when he was five years old. His father was frequently found at the neighborhood bar. Charles and his younger brother and sister were essentially raised by his older sister, who was ten years his elder. Charles never did well at school and had few social skills. His grammar was poor, and he had a difficult time expressing himself.

Katy was raised in a middle-class family. Her parents were semiprofessional. Her father was a workaholic and rarely home. Her mother spent a great deal of time trying to keep up with the Joneses and passed her time shopping for herself, doing volunteer work, and relaxing with friends. She spent very little time with Katy or her older brother John, who was four years her elder. While a teen, John stayed out with his friends most of the time. Katy completed high school and recalls being very good at math.

Charles remembers a household fraught with anger and physical violence. Verbal and physical abuse was normal. The family suffered financially and often received handouts of food and clothing from the local church. Little value was put on education, and the children knew they would be required to leave school and find work as soon as they became of age.

Katy remembers a very quiet, empty home. Her parents and brother were seldom there. She remembers spending endless hours playing make-believe alone with her dolls or being cared for by her elderly and cranky grandmother, who thought nothing of giving her a backhand from time to time. She described herself as lonely and *starved for affection*.

Katy, although Charles's verbal abuse had been present since their first date, never knew how, nor did she have the confidence, to express the hurt she felt. Her grandmother had played a large role in her life, and she was used to getting a backhand slap (comfort zone). She consoled herself in the fact, Charles was a good provider, which fed Katy's need for financial security (comfort zone). At the same time, Katy knew his outbursts would be short-lived, as Charles was seldom home due to the number of overtime hours he worked. Remember, Katy was used to spending time alone (comfort zone) while growing up. Katy also liked the idea of being a wife and being able to care for someone. It fed her need to nurture since she herself felt *starved for affection*.

For almost ten years, Katy enhanced her self-esteem through her job. She developed the social skills required to work with the public, attained a managerial position, and felt good about the way she presented to the public. She was respected by her customers and her boss, who continued to encourage her along a prosperous career path. However, the most important person in her life, the one person she looked to for support,
only called her names and degraded her.

Charles, on the other hand, could not understand why Katy was on the verge of leaving him. He had been raised in a verbally abusive home and had carried this behaviour (comfort zone) into his ten-year marriage without reprisal. He was shocked at his wife's opinions and considered her ungrateful.

For the past ten years, Katy had been working on growing personally, resulting in the celebration of her newly discovered talents and an improved self-esteem which was not willing to suffer the sting of Charles's belittling behaviour. She looked to counselling assistance to help her maintain her newly redefined self and learn new skills with which to communicate with her husband.

Katy came to understand that past behaviours and values (being alone and excessive concern for financial security) learned as a child as a result of circumstances over which *she had no control* were not the behaviours and values she needed as an adult. In other words, financial security did not mean paying the price of living in a lonely marriage, let alone a marriage fraught with verbal abuse.

Charles, through the counselling process, began to understand his learned behaviour (comfort zone) of putting his wife down was his way of building his self-esteem. He had to examine the reasons for his own poor self-esteem. By strengthening his own self-concept and by becoming more accepting of his frailties, he could release himself from the need to abuse and condemn others, which was a destructive defense mechanism. Compassion toward himself would result in compassion toward Katy.

In this case example, we see two people who, as children, were never given the opportunity to build a positive self-concept. Had they, Katy would never have gotten involved with Charles because she would have thought herself more worthy than to be the target of his verbal slandering, and if Charles had developed a more positive self-concept, he would never have had to engage in put-down, name-calling behaviour.

Both were trapped in their own *comfort zones*, making do with values and behaviours well-known to them. They were able to rely on coping skills they had developed years before, which had served them well. The end, unfortunately, outweighed the means, and their negative behaviours became self-perpetuating. Neither had a need or the skills to escape the negative self-perpetuating cycle until Katy began to grow through her job, redefined herself through more positive eyes, and valued herself as someone worthy of a much more loving relationship than the one she was currently experiencing with Charles. Katy had emancipated herself out of her comfort zone. Only then was she able to seek counselling to help her continue her journey of positive self-esteem, knowing all the while her growth may have resulted in the termination of her marriage.

This example demonstrates the correlation between how one's self-concept affects one's ability to communicate well. People with a positive self-concept do not prey on the weaknesses of others. They bolster other people's self-confidence through praise and positive regard, they accept responsibility when they error, they laugh at themselves and are fun to be around. It takes much more effort to be happy than it does to be a passive, powerless victim. The ability to respond (*responsibility*) positively generates more positive energy; misery only attracts more miserable energy. Eleanor Roosevelt once said, "No one can hurt you without your consent." People with healthy self-esteem truly live by this motto. When you learn the language of *self-acceptance*, forgiveness, and approval, you can begin the journey of self-enlightenment and positive self-regard. Remember, it's not your aptitude but your attitude that determines your altitude!

Chapter Three | Why Positive Self-Esteem Is Essential to Effective Communication

People with a negative self-concept fall prey to and even expect to be treated poorly. They engage in talk which consists of "yes … but," "if only …," "there's nothing I can do about it/her/him," "I'll just have to make do," "that's just my luck," "such is life," and so on. These people have learned the language of self-defeat and will, like Katy, choose to stay in an unhappy relationship for ten years because it's comfortable; they know the game rules and know how to respond to them. There is no risk, and there are no challenges. They don't have to muster the courage to grow and change.

Alternatively, there are some people who sabotage their own self-esteem and approval rating in order to reinforce a negative family belief system. As mentioned earlier, I have worked in a group home for teens. The teens constantly referred to themselves as being losers, stupid, or dumb. I asked one young boy why he thought he was dumb. He said he couldn't spell, and due to that, his dad had always called him a dummy. I asked him to list things he could do very well. He said he was good at building model cars and drawing cartoon characters, he was a pretty good goaltender, and he was good at fixing his bicycle. I asked him how someone so dumb could be so good at doing so many things. This perplexed him. He was unable to acknowledge his self-worth because it would mean going against his dad's belief system. It was more important to sabotage his self-esteem than it was to sabotage the parent-child relationship. Is this you?

In addition, there is something I call "the new normal." People who choose to be victims and live in a world of negativity, when pushed to change, will simply make the leap into another unhealthy comfort zone or into a "new normal." For example, Hellen came to me complaining about her current job. She said she was bored, had an overly demanding boss, was underpaid, etc. After weeks of counselling, Hellen decided to stop complaining and take responsibility for her situation. She developed a new resume, began an active job search, and hired a coach to enhance her interview skills. At last, Hellen's efforts were rewarded, and she landed on her dream job. She thought she had really hit the bull's-eye.

Interestingly enough, a few months later, Hellen returned to counselling complaining about her colleagues and the social atmosphere of her new job. She called the women "catty" and "backstabbing." She remarked on their poor dress and poor work ethic. She said her new job was too far from home.

This is a good example of someone creating a negative new normal. Hellen worked hard to get beyond her previous position and in her words "land on her dream job." Once there, however, Hellen could only pick fault with her colleagues, workplace, and commuting time. She wanted to keep herself in the position of victim, sabotaging her personal growth and efforts in improving her career. Her dysfunctional comfort zone won out in the end.

This type of self-deprecating behaviour can continue long after the parents are deceased. My mom is a good example. She had been raised by an absentee mother, who was forced to work long hours in order to support her daughter and unemployed husband. Her father was very punitive and punished her both verbally and physically for the smallest misdemeanor. She was petrified of her father's wrath, yet longed to be loved by him. Her only recourse was to continually say she was sorry and beg for his forgiveness. Mom went through her life apologizing for everything.

When I was in grade 11, my mom visited my sister who was living in Virginia. While she was vacationing, I happened to break my leg when skiing. My dad did not tell her knowing how upsetting this news would be.

Upon mom's return, dad picked her up from the airport and told her they were going to visit a friend in the hospital. He said he wanted it to be a surprise. Mom walked into my room, took one look at the cast, and said, "Oh my God, what have I done?" She obviously felt she had committed some wrongful action which had somehow played a role. Even after both of her parents were deceased, mom still had a need to sustain her parent-child relationship by proving her father right by accepting blame for the accident while at the same time negating her self-worth.

This is not a book about self-esteem. There are many good books which speak to the subject. However, it is important for the purpose of this book that the reader understand the connection between how we see ourselves and how we choose to project ourselves to others. People whose minds are filled with negative *self-talk* will project negative talk. People whose minds are filled with positive *self-talk* will project positive talk.

I support the use of personal mantras. A mantra is a devotional incantation or chant. Mantras are especially useful in helping to build self-esteem, improve relationships, and change personal behaviours. People have been given the gift of a subconscious mind. I have heard our subconscious mind has more information in it than all the libraries in North America. Our subconscious mind is like a steel trap. It remembers everything. Not only does it remember everything it hears, but it also *believes* everything it hears. Invoking a mantra therefore allows the mind to believe and adapt to a new concept or belief system. The constant repetition of the mantra reinforces the new concept. I have seen people change as a result of practicing this simple tool daily even when initially, they don't truly believe in what they are saying.

I suggest clients say their personal mantras either out loud or to themselves a minimum of six times a day. After three weeks, the mind will begin to change and integrate the new information.

For example, every morning when I wake up and as my feet hit the floor, I take a deep breath and say to myself, "I, Patrice McKenzie, will not allow anything or anyone to interfere with my happiness today." I say this mantra over and over while I shower and dress. It works without fail. It's important you put your name into the mantra; otherwise, your subconscious may not know who you are referring to. I also try to say a mantra while doing relaxation breathing. I will not cover relaxation breathing here but will in another chapter.

Depending on your life circumstances, you can create your own personal mantra. A good mantra for improving self-esteem is, "I, [insert first and last name here], am happy and successful. I love myself and am proud of my many gifts and talents. I am not afraid to grow and change as I learn new things about myself and the world I live in."

A mantra I suggest for stress reduction is, "I, [insert first and last name here], am breathing in the universal energy of light, love, health, happiness, and harmony. I am calm and tranquil. I love and respect myself. I will not allow anything or anyone to interfere with my tranquility." I have this mantra printed out on bookmarks so my clients can carry it with them and read it throughout the day.

A good relationship-building mantra is, "I, [insert first and last name here], have a warm and loving relationship with [insert first and last name here]. I trust and believe in him/her and in our mutual ability to respect and nurture each other. I value our togetherness."

A good communications mantra is, "I, [insert first and last name here], am able to speak the truth about who and what I am. I am a good listener and give myself and others the opportunity for complete expression."

Another form of positive self-talk is the *self-affirmation*. Affirmations are statements you make to yourself. For example, "I am okay," "I love myself," "I do not need to punish myself," "I do not have to feel guilty," "I do not have to apologize for things over which I have no control," "I deserve to be loved," "What I think and feel are important," "I am a unique and wonderful person," "I live my life with honesty and integrity," "I set realistic goals for myself," "I can achieve my goals by taking one small step at a time," and so on. By using self-affirmations regularly, both written and verbal, you reprogram your negative self-talk into positive self-talk. This psychological change will translate itself into positive behaviours of self-love and respect.

It is also important to *act* as if you have positive self-esteem even if you haven't achieved it yet. *Fake it until you make it!* Be kind to yourself and act as if you already are the type of person you are working to become. Vision who you want to be in your mind's eye and play that tape over and over again as you go through your day. Compliment yourself (out loud) and others every day. Congratulate yourself when you do something well. Nourish yourself with good food, friends, and exercise. Have fun and, if need be, stop reading the newspaper and listening to the news if it just fills you with sadness. Hellen Keller once said, "The best way out is through." I say, "The best way out is *up*."

You can take the following steps to enhance your self-esteem:

- Recognize your comfort zone and how it may not be working for you.

- Recognize and take care of your needs.

- Use positive, *not* negative, self-talk.

- Accept yourself for who you are.

- Treat yourself and others with kindness and respect.

- Accept positive feedback.

- Live consciously with honesty and integrity.

- Take responsible risks, make decisions, and don't procrastinate.

- Set realistic goals.

- List your strengths and good points and feel comfortable with them.

- Commit to loving yourself: set your goals , write them down, and say them out loud— take action.

- Practice assertiveness: "I'm okay; you're okay."

- Express your feelings honestly without hurting others.

👉 Points to Remember From Chapter Three

- *Self-esteem* can be defined as how much value you place on yourself, or what you think of yourself measured against what you think you should be, or how much you approve or disapprove of yourself measured against your idealized self.

- Self-esteem is determined mainly by the environment in which we were raised.

- Your aim should be to attain a *general* sense of positive self-worth.

- Self-esteem affects everything we do, impacting our life choices, success, and ultimate happiness.

- Negative self-esteem results in unhealthy and self-defeating behaviours, which may be passed on to our children.

- It is important to know what your needs are and how to realize them.

- People have difficulty improving their negative self-esteem because it is too much effort, too scary, or they do not believe themselves worthy of leaving their comfort zones.

- Our comfort zone is where life is predictable, comfortable, and so-called normal even if what goes on in there is unhealthy.

- One's self-concept or self-esteem impacts how we communicate with others.

- People with positive self-esteem do not prey on the weaknesses of others but bolster other people through praise and positive regard. They take responsibility for what they say and are fun to be with.

Points to Remember From Chapter Three

- People with negative self-esteem communicate negatively and have learned the language of self-defeat.

- Anyone harbouring feelings of negative self-worth can achieve positive self-esteem. The use of a personal mantra is a good beginning as well as using positive *self-talk* and *behaving* as if you have positive self-esteem even if you haven't achieved it yet. *Fake it until you make it!*

- Work with a counsellor to enhance your self-esteem.

What Have I Learned From This Chapter That Applies to Me?

What Will I Begin To Do Differently?

Chapter Four
Useful Theories to Understand

In this chapter we will explore a few useful theories to assist in understanding the dynamics of communication. Clients find this helpful because they are able to examine their communications within the context of a theoretical framework that makes sense. Examining your communication in this way allows you to look at it from an objective viewpoint. Having done this, you are able to decide your most appropriate course of action. I will not delve into the complexities of each theory, as that will not serve our purpose, but it is important you gain a general understanding.

Transactional Analysis Theory (TAT)
Transactional analysis theory was developed in the early 1950s. Its simplicity and utility cannot be overstated. It is by far the easiest theory for clients to understand and apply, I have seen this understanding transform individuals almost immediately, resulting in their ability to break out of old patterns and adopt new behaviours and attitudes.

Chapter Four | Useful Theories to Understand

TAT points out we all have three ego states. These ego states are called: child, parent, and adult. Each ego state is important and all healthy people should have and use them.

The *child* ego state is comprised of the thoughts, feelings, and behaviours we bring with us from childhood (age zero to approximately seven) based upon our experiences and upbringing. These years are very important because we develop our self-concept at this time. Further, we bring thoughts, feelings, and behaviours from this time into adulthood.

A child raised in a nurturing, healthy environment will grow to be creative, spontaneous and fun loving, and bask in feelings of positive self-regard. A child that has been neglected, however, will grow up with a negative self-image with all the characteristic accompanying feelings we addressed in chapter three.

Also, keep in mind that during this time there are a few years where you have not yet learned to speak. This does not mean you did not have thoughts and feelings. It means your thoughts and feelings where pre-language interpretations, which may be right or wrong but, nonetheless, were true to you. These truths, write and wrong, are carried into adulthood and also comprise the child ego state.

The *parent* ego state mirrors the way we saw our parents' behave toward us. In other words, we bring with us our parents' rules, for example, the shoulds and should nots. If we had very punitive, directive, authoritative parents, we too will have a more directive, authoritative parent ego state. If our parents were more laissez-faire, then we too will develop a more laissez- faire parent ego state. In addition, our values are born from our parent ego.

The *adult* ego state speaks to our ability to take responsibility to understand information, analyze the information realistically, and make our own sound decisions. Based on those decisions, we can then take appropriate action. The *adult* is more concerned with facts than feelings.

It is important to understand all three ego states are essential to a healthy personality. The child in us allows us the freedom to romp and play with our own children and friends, the parent ego sets some predictable guidelines around how we choose to live, and the adult ego state helps us to evaluate information, make good decisions, and do the right thing.

When two people engage in a communication, they are *transacting*, thus the name transactional analysis therapy. However, when two people communicate, they each have three ego states available to them from which to speak. The magic to effective communication is to ensure you are coming from your appropriate ego state given the situation and the person with whom you are communicating, thereby complementing your mutual ego states.

Dysfunctional communication often occurs when one person adopts an ego state from which to communicate, which is inconsistent with the ego state from which the other person is coming. In a marriage, for example, the optimum condition is both partners communicating essentially from their adult ego states. However, it is not uncommon for a woman to marry a childlike man because the relationship reinforces the woman's own parent ego state and her need to nurture. It is not uncommon to find a man who marries a childlike woman because it reinforces his punitive parent ego state, which may be to control and dominate. Again, everyone's ego states are defined by and dependent upon their own personal experiences while growing up.

Here are some examples:

Parent Role
"Hello, neighbour. I am having a BBQ tomorrow. I know you have difficulty controlling your children. I would appreciate it if you could try and keep them quiet while my guests are here."

Child Role (Victim)
"Hello, neighbour. My husband and I have been suffering next door as a result of the loud music, screaming, and yelling of your children and their friends. I tell you, there is just no peace around here. I can't even think about having friends over for a BBQ. You are forcing us to consider moving."

Adult Role
"Hello, neighbour. Tomorrow evening my husband and I are having a BBQ. I know your children and their friends enjoy your pool and behave like children having fun, just as I did when I was their age. Could you please let them know we are having guests over tomorrow so they can keep the noise down a bit? Thanks, neighbour."

Chapter Four | Useful Theories to Understand

🔍 The Case of Ellen

While completing my master's degree, I did a practicum placement at a counselling service agency. I was assigned Ellen, a new client. She had made an appointment to see a therapist about issues relating to her marriage. Ellen was thirty-seven years old and had been married for over twelve years. She had two children. She presented as a very bright individual and was immaculately dressed in an electric blue suit, white blouse, and black patent leather pumps. Her hair was quite stylish. The articulation of her concerns was done brilliantly in a forthright and capable manner. She was confident and projected positive self esteem. She was objective and well balanced in her interpretation of the issues. She had a very pleasant, amicable, mature way about her. At the end of the session, I suggested her husband join us the following week.

I was greeted the next week by both Ellen and her husband, Rod. He was forty-two years old, sporting a navy blue pin-striped suit and carrying a briefcase. I'm not sure why he brought the briefcase with him, as he didn't use it during our visit. He was pleasant and seemed genuinely concerned over the health of their marriage. He answered questions with both frankness and sincerity.

As I was conversing with Rod, I began to notice some obvious changes taking place in Ellen. To begin, her posture did not reflect the confident erect posture of last week. To the contrary, Ellen was slumped in her chair, head falling forward with her arms crossed against her chest, and legs crossed at the knees and pulled toward her torso. She looked as though she were trying to make herself appear very small. She looked down at the floor or out of the window. When I spoke to Ellen, I was even more taken aback by the newly found resonance to her voice. Her forthright presentation of seven days ago had been replaced by a high-pitched, soft, baby like voice. Ellen's transformation was astounding. That, coupled with my novice experience at the time, led me to think she was playing a joke. To my utter disbelief, the behaviour remained consistent throughout the session.

It was clear Ellen adopted her *child* ego state when in the company of her husband. She became weak, frail, indecisive, and dependent. I later learned Ellen often engaged in acting out behaviour in the company of her husband that included temper tantrums and long spells of crying. Ellen longed to be parented. However, her husband had no intention of being her parent but longed for and missed the wife he once knew, or thought he knew as an adult.

In this example, Ellen was demonstrating inappropriate dependency as a result of her inability to successfully integrate her child ego state into her overall persona. The child ego state had become the dominant personality in her marriage, which led to dysfunctional communication between her and her husband. Upon closer examination, I learned while they were dating, Ellen thought Rod was her knight in shining armor. He was self-assured, self-directed, and represented stability. Rod fell in love with Ellen because she reminded him of everything he was not. She was playful, always laughing, and having fun. She was easy to get along with because she would follow his lead, and did everything in her power to please him. Ellen was a bit shy and needed the steady arm of Rod around her, which bolstered his self-esteem.

In the long run, and after twelve years of marriage, Rod became dissatisfied with having a child for a wife and acted accordingly. Rod didn't want to be a parent to Ellen and responded to her with frustration. Ellen, on the other hand, felt rejected, and inasmuch as she did everything she could to please him, her every effort just seemed to annoy Rod even more.

The goal of counselling was to assist Ellen to integrate all of her ego states appropriately and to assist her in discovering why her child ego state dominated her marital relationship.

Over the years, I have also seen relationships breakdown because one partner slowly regresses back into an inappropriate ego state.

The Case of Pete and Lori

Pete and Lori had been married for ten years. They described themselves as having a stable relationship up until the previous year at which time Pete became involved with another woman, Debbie. Pete claimed he had always felt an emotional distance between himself and Lori and found the other woman gave him the emotional support and caring he needed.

Chapter Four | Useful Theories to Understand

This came as quite a surprise to Lori, who had no idea Pete had perceived her as being emotionally distant and non caring. Lori described their marriage as being one of give and take, where issues were discussed and negotiated, and fairness prevailed. Lori described herself as the planner, organizing most of their affairs, including finances, holidays, household tasks, and personal social engagements. She excelled at administrative tasks. Pete went along with this arrangement, recognizing that organization was not his strong suit. Over time, however, Pete translated this as a distancing behaviour because of the increasing amount of time Lori was forced to spend attending to so many administrative tasks as their family grew. Pete did not offer to help or learn how to do the tasks or speak with Lori about his feelings. He chose to withdraw.

Being an outgoing person, Lori was involved in some community organizations and events-planning committees. Over the years, she had encouraged Pete to participate in similar community activities. Pete responded by getting involved with volunteer work. He initially found it satisfying. Over time, however, he bemoaned the amount of time they spent away from each other as a result of these extracurricular activities. He translated this into feelings of aloneness and abandonment, which was reminiscent of his childhood.

When Pete met Debbie (who had just separated from her husband), he, in his child ego state, was delighted to fall into the arms of a *parent* ego state which was quite willing to focus solely on him and attend to his insatiable hunger for personal and emotional attention and support. It is not surprising this relationship was short-lived, as Debbie soon began to regret having to be Pete's parent.

In Pete and Lori's relationship, we find a wife who works primarily from her *adult* ego state. She was attracted to Pete because he was calm, quiet, and responsible. She was attracted to him intellectually and concurred with his family values. He was fun to be with, which complemented her more serious side. Pete was attracted to Lori because she was able to keep his life uncomplicated and he admired her "take charge" approach. He admired her many capabilities. Through therapy, Pete realized he had been looking for a mom in Lori and was ultimately able to reevaluate some of his earlier choices and behaviours and work at becoming a better *adult* partner with her.

Again, keep in mind it is important we acknowledge and respect all three ego states. In doing so, we acknowledge who we are in our entirety - we acknowledge our authentic selves. We can look honestly at each ego state and better understand ourselves by understanding them and how they were developed. We can find great joy in expressing all our ego states because we have integrated them properly. Parents and grandparents love enjoying their *child* ego states with their children and grandchildren. Likewise, they are able to function from their *parent* ego state when needed, but the goal is to stay primarily in their *adult* ego state when communicating with adults.

The Case of Nan

"I can't say I was that lucky in my first marriage. Despite the fact we were not suitably matched in a lot of ways and I married too young and married for all the wrong reasons, both my ex-husband and I did not have strong adult ego states. I believe I contributed to the failing of our marriage by toggling between my child and parent ego states. I had never lived on my own. When I married, I dragged my child ego state into my marriage because my parents had not demonstrated, taught, or encouraged me to develop an adult ego state. They were either emotionally or physically absent or punitive and judgmental when they were present. Given I had no experience with an adult ego state, I thought being a good wife meant being either obedient or nurturing. As such, I did most of the thinking, planning and supporting resulting in an imbalance in our relationship."

Also note that people who have a history of dysfunctional relationships usually continue to attract people who will satisfy their inappropriate ego state. For example, adults who like to function from their child ego state will probably attract people who like to function from their parent ego state and vise versa. These people will usually sabotage healthy relationships because healthy relationships fail to feed their predominant ego state. Unfortunately, this pattern will remain cyclical until the individual can break the pattern by making friends with all their ego states and learning to use them wisely. Therapy can be very useful in making this discovery.

Try to think of a relationship you have had which didn't work out. Examine the roles assumed by yourself and the other individual. Look to identify the predominant ego states used by both of you and examine how these ego states coexisted (or didn't). If it helps, draw a diagram of each of you and script a verbal interaction using arrows from your ego state to the other person. You will find this exercise very informative.

Reality Therapy

Reality therapy was developed in 1980. Its basic premise states all behaviour is derived by people striving to meet common basic needs, for example, to love, to be loved, to feel good about yourself, and to be liked by others. However, reality therapy states people must *learn* how to satisfy their needs. We do this based on (once again) how we have been raised. If a person has been raised in a loving and supportive environment, the individual will learn responsible behaviours with which to meet their own needs and communicate their needs clearly. For example, if a child is raised believing they are kind, they will probably behave like a kind person as an adult. If a child has been raised to believe they are not worthy or perhaps even worthless, they, as an adult, may believe they have no need to act or communicate responsibly.

Reality therapy speaks to the three Rs: right, responsible, and real. Doing what is *right* is doing what is normally accepted. Being *responsible* is the ability to look after your own needs without hurting anyone else. *Real* means being able to see the world as most people see it.

So what does this have to do with communication? Within this framework effective communication is the process by which you are able to satisfy *your* needs. In addition, it is important to remember effective communication will result because you *act responsibly*. Conversely, a miscommunication will result and your needs will not be met when you have failed to take personal responsibility for the communications process.

🔍 The Case of Rose (Mom) and Lily (Daughter)

Rose came to counselling because she was having difficulty communicating and getting along with her eighteen-year-old daughter. Lily was in her final year of high school, was undecided about her direction the following year, and had recently broken up with her boyfriend. Rose also had a twenty-year-old daughter, Samantha, living away from home and doing very well at university. Rose and Samantha had always had a good relationship, and she was finding Samantha's absence difficult, which was only compounded by Lily's daily "foul mouth" and "unbelievable behaviour." Rose had been separated from her husband for five years.

I requested Lily join us in counselling. Lily agreed. She was a very attractive young woman, tall with blue eyes, and long blond hair. Her face was fixed into a determined grimace, lips in a snarl and eyes pinched. She resembled a frightened animal. I purposely asked her to sit in the chair closest to the door, as to not enhance her feelings of being trapped or cornered.

I began the session by thanking Lily for joining us and reviewing her mom's reasons for coming to counselling. I spoke to her mom's goal to improve the relationship between her and Lily. I asked Lily if she was willing to participate in improving the relationship as well. Lily gave a reluctant and suspicious yes. I explained my role in the process before proceeding.

I began by asking Rose to express her thoughts and feelings about the relationship. A reoccurring theme in Rose's description was Lily's name-calling and blaming. Apparently, Lily would blame Rose if she was late for school, lost her keys, couldn't find any clean clothes to wear, got sick, had a fight with her boyfriend, and didn't have any money, and so on. While Rose was speaking, I had to stop Lily from interrupting with ferocious outbursts of name-calling toward her mom.

After a couple of visits, Lily was more comfortable and agreed to an individual counselling session. Lily expressed her feelings of failure, low self-worth, and fear of moving forward with her life. I was then able to focus on Lily's angry outbursts and behaviour toward her mom, which she acknowledged. I asked, "If you had to stop blaming your mom for your actions, what would that mean?" I referenced Rose's earlier comments about being blamed for Lily being late for school. Lily was reluctant at first, but with the assistance of some compassionate encouragement, Lily was able to say, "If I had to stop blaming my mom for being late for school, it would mean I would have to set my alarm or maybe two alarms to make sure I would get up in the morning, I would have to go to bed earlier so I wouldn't sleep in, I would have to stop drinking so much coffee so I would sleep better, I would have to eat well because I always wake up in the middle of the night feeling hungry and then can't get back to sleep."

Chapter Four | Useful Theories to Understand

Lily was then able to answer the question, If you had to stop blaming your mom for you always losing your keys, what would it mean? Lily was able to complete her own list with ease, including, "If I had to stop blaming my mom for me losing my keys, it would mean always putting them in my purse when I am out, always hanging them up in the same place when I return home, and never loaning them to friends." Lily was then able to go through each of the areas where she had laid blame onto Rose.

Through this process, Lily was able to discover her need to become responsible for her communications and actions, which would then erase her need to verbally abuse her mom. She learned that blaming behaviour was self-pitying, and did not allow her to grow up and get on with her life. She also understood blaming behaviour was destructive as it prevented her from having a healthy relationship with her mom. She had used blaming behaviour in an effort to make her mom feel guilty. The act of becoming responsible and doing the right thing would ultimately change Lily's behaviour and communication style resulting in improved relationships and positive self-esteem.

Perhaps you can see yourself in Rose or Lily and how your responses may negatively effect your communication with others. It is essential you do not wallow in self-guilt, but take positive action to regain your self worth. You can do this by contracting with yourself to change. In other words, examine how you speak to others and evaluate your *purpose*. Are your intentions to hurt the other person, make them feel guilty, or abdicate responsibility? If so, contract with yourself to take responsibility and change your communications style accordingly. Remember, effective communication means having the *ability to respond*. Be prepared to take baby steps. Change does not happen in giant leaps. Don't accept your own excuses. If you do not succeed, develop another plan and contract with yourself again. Make sure your plan is achievable; don't sabotage your success. Don't punish yourself if you don't succeed all of the time; believe in your intention to do better. And lastly, congratulate yourself for all your finer qualities.

In the case of Rose and Lily, Lily was an exceptional instrumentalist and had played in the city's youth orchestra for a number of years. In that capacity, she had won an opportunity to travel internationally. Lily had to learn to accept her gift and congratulate herself for being such an accomplished musician. Rose, too, had to learn to send more positive messages to Lily to enhance Lily's esteem and reinforce Lily's desire to change.

The concepts of reality therapy are especially helpful when communicating with children and youth. It is essential children and youth learn to take responsibility for what they say and do. A responsible individual is a happy individual and will not grow into adulthood carrying a false concept of their reality.

The Case of Dora and Phillip

Dora and Phillip had been married for nine years. They had no children. They had been experiencing marital difficulties for two years. Phillip was a demanding husband. Phillip, because his overly demanding position kept him occupied almost seven days a week, insisted Dora be responsible for everything else in their lives. Dora took care of the cooking; cleaning; shopping; laundry; Christmas and birthday gift buying; family gatherings; setting dental appointments; hair and doctor's appointments; car servicing, lawn cutting and snow removal; making the vacation plans; and doing their mutual packing. Dora also planned his wardrobe and picked out his clothes for the following day before she went to bed each night. Oh, and did I forget to tell you, Dora was a full-time dental hygienist?

Dora came to counselling complaining of her husband's demanding, authoritative behaviour. She was exhausted from carrying out all her duties and disliked being his "servant." She said Phillip had become emotionally and physically "distant," ignored her when they did have time together and spoke to her abrasively.

For example, Dora made dinner reservations to take Phillip's parents out to celebrate their anniversary. The reservations included Dora and Phillip, her parents-in-law, Phillip's two brothers, and their respective wives. She coordinated the date and time of the dinner, chose the location, arranged transportation for Phillip's parents, and ordered a bouquet of her mother-in-law's favourite flowers for the occasion. She also bought Phillip a new shirt and tie for the evening. She wanted everything to be just perfect. When Dora asked Phillip if he liked his new shirt and tie, he replied with, "Yea, so what?"

Now, before we start berating Phillip for what he said, let's take a look at

Chapter Four | Useful Theories to Understand

the things over which Dora had control; after all, it is Dora who came for counselling. If we were looking at this relationship through the glasses of a transactional analysis therapist, we would have to ask Dora why she wanted and needed to be Phillip's parent. We would have to ask Phillip why he wanted and needed to be Dora's child. If we were looking at this dynamic through the glasses of a reality therapist, we would have to ask Dora what it would mean if she couldn't blame Phillip any more for her unhappiness. We would ask Dora to examine her pattern of behaviour and communication with Phillip to determine why she invited Phillip to treat her like a servant. Where was the reward?

Dora discovered she had always been a good *helper* because it bolstered her self-esteem. It made her feel worthwhile and loved. She would even help others if it meant putting herself last after everyone else's needs were met. Her vocabulary comprised of *yes, of course, I'd be glad to do it, you can count on me, and it's no bother at all*. Dora said these things despite it not being a true reflection of her inner wants and needs. She projected a false self to the world and to herself. She was not living by the three Rs of *right*, *responsible*, and *real*.

When we explored Dora's relationship with Phillip, Dora learned a few things about herself. To begin, Dora had felt unloved as a child which turned her into a pleaser. Pleasing others gave her the attention she needed. Feeling unloved as a child also left Dora feeling unworthy resulting in her becoming a passive participant in life, and possibly in her marriage as well. To assert herself and regain a sense of self worth Dora took control over Phillip by planning his existence thus making herself the servant. Dora acknowledged her behaviour went against satisfying her own needs and was not right, responsible or real to a healthy marriage.

Although Dora couldn't change the way Phillip communicated with her, she contracted to change herself and the way she communicated with Phillip and others. This discovery of her own self worth was Dora's epiphany, which she expressed in tearful glory. There is nothing better than the cleansing sound of one's sobbing to the silent sound of self-awareness.

Dora adopted a new language, which included, "No, I'm afraid I am unable to help you, but I might be able to recommend someone who can," "I can understand your predicament, but I'm sure you can see your way clear," "I'd like to take a pass on this one," "I'd like to hear your ideas and see how we can work together," "What suggestions do you have?" "I'll prioritize my things-to-do list and then get back to you," "I am responsible for my own happiness," "I am responsible for my relationship with Phillip, which means I must confront my fears of not being loved and communicate with him from my powerful adult self."

Behaviour or Learning Theory

Behaviour or learning theorists believe our behaviour is solely dependent upon our environment, and our behaviour is determined by the responses we receive from those around us. Further, they promote our personalities are developed based on the three laws of learning. These laws include classical conditioning, operant conditioning, and imitative learning. For the purpose of understanding how communicating more effectively fits into this theory, it is only necessary to understand the basic concepts of each.

Classical conditioning states you can have a neuromuscular and glandular response based on some event that is going on around you. This is also known as a conditioned reflex. Most of you will be familiar with Ivan Pavlov and his salivating dogs. Pavlov coupled the feeding of his dogs to the sound of a bell. Before long, the dogs would salivate (respond) upon hearing the sound of the bell even though there was no food present. The dogs were conditioned to salivate to the sound of the bell because they had *learned* to associate the bell (stimuli) with being fed.

Operant conditioning has nothing to do with stimuli but states a person's behaviour will be repeated based upon the outcome of having performed that behaviour before. The outcome (positive or negative) will determine if the behaviour will be repeated. For example, when my son was a little boy, I asked him to hold the door open for me as I approached with an armload of groceries. I thanked him, gave him a hug, and told him how much I appreciated him helping me and how kind I thought he was. The following week when I returned from grocery shopping, my son said, "Wait, Mom, I'll hold the door." My son didn't have to be asked to hold the door open for me because he had *learned* that doing so, would result in receiving praise and a hug.

Imitative learning states people do not learn behaviours based on the consequences of their past behaviours, but believe we can learn by imitating someone else. For example, when I was doing a practicum placement, I imitated some successful techniques used by the supervisor to elicit like responses from my clients.

Another important concept to behaviour theory is the concept of reinforcement. There are a number of reinforcements that can determine behaviour such as money, love, adoration and belonging. For example, if you help a friend with a task, you will receive a feeling of positive self worth and a heart felt thanks from your friend. Due to these positive responses to your behaviour you will likely repeat your behaviour in the future.

Other, less pleasant reinforcers which can also determine behaviour include things like ridicule, blaming and name-calling. For example, if you are yelled at after performing a task, chances are you will not perform that task again.

All is to say behaviour or learning theorists believe that behaviour is determined by the type of reinforcement you have previously received. Now we can begin relating this theory into learning to communicate more effectively.

Let's begin with the theory of *classical conditioning*:

"I can't go to school today, Mommy, because my tummy's sick," says six-year-old Scott who physically trembled at the thought of going to school. His mother soon learned Scott had been punched by a new boy at school for not giving the boy his dessert at lunch time. Scott became physically ill (response) because he associated school with being punched (stimuli) and therefore didn't want to go. The goal here is to teach Scot to use his words to communicate his fears and the events that led to him being afraid.

Operant conditioning is perhaps the simplest tool to assist you in communicating effectively. To review, my son repeated the behaviour of opening the door for me upon my return from grocery shopping because he knew he would receive praise for doing so. The consequence of his behaviour led to him to receive positive feedback; thus, it was repeated. Conversely, if I had scolded him and said he did not do a good job of opening the door the likelihood of him repeating the behaviour would be slim.

"Ever since I began a weekly employee-recognition program at work," says the manager of a large automobile company, "my employees have had fewer sick days, sales have improved, employee complaints have almost disappeared, and the staff seems to get along a lot better." A mother of a teenage daughter says jubilantly, "Ever since I began telling Julie I trusted her to set her own guidelines around curfew and study time, she has been coming home earlier than usual, and her grades have improved." A surprised dad offers, "My son Todd started working six months ago. I didn't think he would last at the job very long. The work certainly isn't something that interests him. However, his boss seems to have taken a shine to him and is giving him more responsibility. It makes Todd feel great, and he is really excelling. I'm proud of him." The professor of a master's of counselling program says, "I've finally figured out how to get the most out of the students. I bring a paper bag of five or six treats to each class, including chips, chocolate bars, and one can of beer. At the end of class, I throw the goodies out to the students who have contributed the most. The students love it, especially the can of beer!"

On the other hand, parents who remove privileges from their children after behaving poorly are also employing the techniques of operant conditioning. The consequence of having privileges removed will act as a deterrent to having the offending behaviour repeated.

These examples provide easy proof that operant conditioning is a useful tool when communicating. We all want to love and be loved and will act in ways to ensure these needs are satisfied. To that end, your communications with others can respond to that need.

With regard to imitative learning always ensure you present as a good role model, a role model whose behaviour and communications are worthy of imitating. I have seen numerous adolescents who have vocabularies straight out of the gutter. When I met their parents, I got a firsthand look at the original gutter diggers.

Chapter Four | Useful Theories to Understand

My grandmother used to say "all you come into the world with is your name. So it's very important to honour your name in what you do and say because it is the only thing that you will be remembered by".

Individual Psychology

Alfred Adler was a practicing physician from Vienna who came to the United States in 1926. Although he was a student/colleague of Freud, Adler developed his own ideas about psychoanalysis and developed the field of *individual psychology*. Adler believed that because people are social beings, we have a sense of social responsibility. He also taught that people have a natural ability to move forward in their lives by setting goals to be achieved, thus moving them forward and making their world a better place. Unlike behaviour theory, Adler believed people are self-determining. In other words, people can choose their own behaviour and communications based upon what they individually want to achieve and, further to that, choose how they are going to get there. You may be familiar with the term *self-determinism*.

Adler suggests that by the time a child is five years old, s/he has developed behaviours based on how s/he perceives of the world. It is these behaviours, good or bad, that we take into adulthood. Adler calls this entire package of behaviours our lifestyle. Furthermore, we may not know why or even like the way we are behaving as adults because we did not have the vocabulary or cognitive ability to figure that out when we first developed the behaviours as small children. This is where the assistance of a therapist comes in handy.

The good thing about individual psychology is that it advocates self-determinism. Since behaviours and the subsequent way we communicate are learned, we can unlearn the unhealthy behaviours we learned as infants and children and replace them with healthier behaviours and ways of communicating. We do not have to be dependent upon our environment and play the role of passive recipient.

For example, if we go back and look at Scot's case within the context of classical conditioning, we can say the *thought* of seeing the bully causes Scot to panic, resulting in a stomach ache. The *thought* is the stimulus. The stomach ache is the response.

However, within the context of individual psychology, Scot can be taught to speak with his parents or teacher and communicate his thoughts and feelings thus putting him in a position of strength. He will also learn to remove himself from bothersome individuals to avoid becoming the victim.

Individual psychology also advocates "When you receive a stimulus, you do not have to respond immediately." There can be quite a lapse of time between the stimulus and your response. In fact, you can choose not to respond at all. Keep in mind no response is a response.

Stimulus $\longrightarrow$ **Choice** $\longrightarrow$ **Response**

I remind clients about the stimulus / response option when they speak of having their buttons pushed or being hooked. We all have buttons which can be pushed, and people who know us well seem to know where to find them.

Buttons can be pushed during the most casual conversations or during heated discussions or arguments and are usually used to hurt someone. I do not advocate the use of this behaviour, but I can give some counsel around what to do when you are on the receiving end.

First of all, be prepared. I am always on guard with a response. Second, don't take ownership over someone else's poor behaviour. Always ask yourself *first*: "Whose problem is this anyway?" If they want to say cruel, hurtful things, it is their problem and not yours. Third, people say hurtful things to make themselves feel more superior. By responding with anger, you only feed into their need to win, and you may be reinforcing their attitude about you if they think you are a lesser person. Next, remember no response is a response, and if necessary, physically remove yourself from the situation.

I counsel a number of separated people. A pet peeve of clients is how easily riled they get when they hear from or see their ex-spouse. Ex-spouses know what buttons to push and at times push them liberally. You may be familiar with the inevitable phone call that comes when you least expect it. It starts with something like this, "Hi, Alice, it's me. Can you talk, or is that boy toy of yours visiting?" or "Hi, John, it's Tracy. I know you have difficulty controlling the children, but could you keep them at bay long enough to hear what I'm calling about?" or "Hi, Sam, it's me. Because you don't seem to want to learn how to cook, I thought the children could visit you after I have fed them dinner," or "If you can get over playing the poor ex-wife, I need to talk to you about finances." The list goes on and on and on.

For calls or conversations of this nature, you must remember the all-important word: *choice*. You have a choice regarding (a) if you respond and (b) if so, how you respond. You are self-determining and not a puppet on the end of someone's string.

I often suggest clients keep a recipe card by the phone that has a couple of sound responses printed on them. Responses can vary given the subject and tone of the incoming statement. If someone is being rude toward you or shouting, your response can be, "When you are prepared to speak to me properly, I would be more than willing to discuss X with you. Phone me back when you are prepared to do that. I am hanging up the phone now, good-bye," or "I commit to speaking to you with respect, and I expect that in return. Phone me back when you can communicate with me more civilly, good-bye" or "I choose not to participate in this shouting match, please phone back when you have calmed down, good-bye."

If necessary, you can use the same responses over and over again. Consistency is important to success. However, if this does not remedy the situation, finding an alternate form of communication (e-mail, written notes, etc.), or not responding at all, are available options. Often, e-mail is very effective between people because you can remove the emotion and keep to the facts. You also have a record of your communication.

👉 Points to Remember From Chapter Four

- Understanding a few simple theories will assist you in better understanding the dynamics of your communication and why people do what they do.
- Once you understand the theories, you can apply them to your own situation, enabling you to break out of old patterns and adopt new behaviours and attitudes.

Transactional analysis theory (TAT) speaks to everyone having three ego states—child, parent, and adult. When people communicate, they *transact* from one of these states.

- Each ego state is healthy providing there is *balance*. Unhealthy or dysfunctional communication happens when either the parent or child ego states predominate.
- The ideal relationship is when both parties primarily communicate from their adult ego states.

Reality theory states people's behaviour is determined by people striving to meet basic needs.

- Reality theory states people *learn* how to go about satisfying these needs based on how we have been raised.
- If you have been raised in a loving, supportive environment, you will learn responsible behaviours and ways to communicate to meet your needs. If you have been raised in a negative or deprived environment, the need to act and communicate responsibly is lessened.
- Reality theory speaks to the three Rs: right, responsible, and real. All individuals should do what is right according to what most view as acceptable, be responsible, be able to look after their own needs without hurting others, and know their reality is also the reality shared by all.

Chapter Four | Useful Theories to Understand

👉 Points to Remember From Chapter Four

- Miscommunication occurs when you fail to live up to or abide by the three Rs.

Behaviour or learning theory believes we are solely dependent upon what goes on around us and our behaviour is determined by the responses we receive from our environment.

- Behaviour theory contends our personalities are developed based on the three laws of learning - classical conditioning, operant conditioning, and imitative learning.
- We can apply these three laws of learning in how we choose to communicate. In other words, we can provide positive and supportive feed back.

Individual psychology states people are driven by a sense of social responsibility, we have a need to move forward with our lives by achieving set goals, and we have a need to make the world a better place.

- Individual psychology believes in *self-determination*, which means people can choose their own goals, and behave and communicate in a distinct way in order to fulfill them.
- Individual psychology states our behaviour and communications are based on how we have perceived the world while growing up - good or bad / right or wrong.
- The good thing about individual psychology is we can unlearn unhealthy behaviours and communications and replace them with healthier approaches.
- People have a *choice* on how they choose to best respond.

Useful Theories to Understand | Chapter Four

What Have I Learned From This Chapter That Applies to Me?

Chapter Four | Useful Theories to Understand

✎ What Will I Begin To Do Differently?

Chapter Five
The Who and Why of Communication

If we review chapter one, I spoke about how easy it is to speak with a friend. The *who* is very important in communication, as it determines our level of comfort and also the care with which we present our words. The *why* is equally important because it helps us understand our feelings. Who do you find most easy and most difficult to communicate with and why? People that are easy to communicate with are generally people with whom we get along well, who have no hidden agendas, and who care about our well-being. People with whom we have difficulty communicating are usually people who do not know us very well, could be out to hurt us, and don't care about our well being. However, there are always exceptions to the rule. Sometimes family is more difficult to communicate with than our boss or a police officer who has just stopped us for a traffic violation.

It is important to recognize with whom you have the greatest difficulty speaking. Make a list of significant people with whom you communicate. Assign each name a number one through 10, the number one representing the *most* difficult to speak with up to the number 10, the *least* difficult to speak with. How many fall within the number one to three categories, how many fall in the middle range, and how many fall within seven to 10? Hopefully you have more higher numbers than lower numbers. However, if you don't, that's okay too. Remember, new behaviours are easily learned. Now, beside each name write down the associated thoughts and then feelings you get when speaking with this person and *why* you get this feeling. Let's have a look at Mary's table.

Significant People With Whom Mary Communicates

Person	Mother	Father
Rating (1-10)	6	9
1st thoughts I get when communicating	• I'm liked only as long as I make her feel good about herself.	• I love Dad. • He respects me. • I'm lucky to have him as my father.
Feeling(s) I get when I communicate with this person	• uncomfortable • anxious	• unconditionally loved • happy, joyful • supported
Why I get these feelings	• She judges me and compares me to other people. • She talks a lot about herself and doesn't seem to care about what is going on in my life. • She seems angry a lot of the time.	• I am listened to completely. • He is physically affectionate. • I can be myself around him. • He makes me laugh.

The Who and Why of Communication | *Chapter Five*

Significant People With Whom Mary Communicates

Person	Husband	Sister
Rating (1-10)	10	5
1st thoughts I get when communicating	· I love being with my husband. · I am one lucky woman.	· I am barely liked by her.
Feeling(s) I get when I communicate with this person	· loved · happy · safe · comfortable/relaxed · respected · trusted	· angry · betrayed · annoyed
Why I get these feelings	· I can say and do anything, and I know I am still loved. · He is attentive to all my needs. · He is verbally and physically affectionate. · He knows how to make me feel better. · He listens to my point of view and respects me.	· She likes to pick fights. · She makes rude comments about my husband and son. · She acts like a snob. · She lies to me sometimes.

Chapter Five | The Who and Why of Communication

Significant People With Whom Mary Communicates

Person	Boss	16 year old Son
Rating (1-10)	4	5-7
1st thoughts I get when communicating	· I do not like him as a person.	· He is having a hard time growing up. · I'm doing my best to help and love him.
Feeling(s) I get when I communicate with this person	· angry · frustrated	· loved most of the time · angry · suspicious · anxious
Why I get these feelings	· He is dictatorial. · He is patronizing. · He doesn't listen to anyone's opinions but his own.	· He can be very affectionate. · He has outbursts that are very upsetting. · He has lied to me about where he is and who he is with. · I can't always trust him and that makes me worry.

Significant People With Whom Mary Communicates

Person	Ex-Husband	Close Friend
Rating (1-10)	3	8-9
1st thoughts I get when communicating	• I really do not like him or his behaviour. • I think I am unsafe around him.	• I am so lucky to have her in my life. • She's great!
Feeling(s) I get when I communicate with this person	• angry • guilty • disgusted • confused • afraid	• loved • happy • trusted
Why I get these feelings	• He is insulting. • He likes to pick fights. • He wants revenge. • He is selfish and doesn't care about our son the way I'd like him to.	• She listens to me when I'm sad and tries to help me put things into perspective. • She is very funny. • She is physically affectionate. • She tells me her most intimate secrets.

Chapter Five | The Who and Why of Communication

Significant People With Whom Mary Communicates

Person	Therapist	Night School Teacher
Rating (1-10)	8	5
1st thoughts I get when communicating	• I like her, and I think she likes me. • She is a good listener.	• She is a hard woman to figure out. • I think she likes me.
Feeling(s) I get when I communicate with this person	• safe • unconditionally cared for	• uncomfortable • anxious
Why I get these feelings	• She is quiet and calm. • She doesn't interrupt me. • She offers helpful insight. • I can tell her anything without fear of rejection. • She is very professional.	• She is aloof. • She can be a bit abrupt, and sometimes I think she doesn't have time for my questions. • Sometimes I feel stupid around her.

Significant People With Whom Mary Communicates

Person	Natural Health Care Practitioner	Personal Trainer
Rating (1-10)	8	7
1st thoughts I get when communicating	• She/he is well trained. • She/he is helping me. • She/he likes me.	• She/he is well trained. • She/he is helping me. • She/he likes me.
Feeling(s) I get when I communicate with this person	• liked • attended to • comfortable • relaxed	• happy • attended to • comfortable
Why I get these feelings	• She is caring and listens to my concerns. • She thinks about my health holistically. • She is very professional. • Her approach is open and non threatening.	• She/he is funny. • She/he really knows his trade. • She/he appears to sincerely want to help me achieve my fitness goals.

If we take a look at Mary's thoughts and feelings when she is communicating with those she feels *least* comfortable, we find a common thread. Her thoughts include disliked, unsafe, and confused. Mary's feelings include discomfort, anxiety, and anger. When we look at why Mary has these feelings, we observe the following: dictatorial, insulting, lying and angry behaviours, disregard for her thoughts and feelings, and being judged.

If we look at Mary's thoughts when she is communicating with those she feels *most* comfortable, her thoughts include the following: being liked, loved, trusted, and respected. If we look at Mary's feelings when she is communicating with those she feels *most* comfortable, we also find a common thread. These feelings include happiness, safety, and comfort. When we look at why Mary has these feelings, we observe the following: attentive listening behaviours, receiving physical affection, being respected, having fun, laughing and being dealt with in a professional manner.

This is a useful exercise for Mary for two reasons. To begin, Mary can compare her thoughts and feelings against *why* she has those thoughts and feelings. In other words, is Mary justified in feeling angry, betrayed, and annoyed at her sister given her sister likes to pick fights, make rude comments, lies, and acts like a snob? It is important to do reality checks on ourselves to ensure our thoughts and feelings are congruent to the occasion. We can also take the exercise one step further and examine Mary's behaviour when she is in the company of those with whom she communicates least well.

The following is an example:

People with Whom Mary Does Not Feel Comfortable Communicating	Mary's Behaviour When She Is with This Person
Mother (6)	quiet, on guard
Sister (5)	standoffish, aloof
Ex-husband (3)	evasive, shy
Boss (4)	shy, apprehensive, withdrawn
Night-School Teacher (5)	quiet, adolescent

This is a good exercise because it gives Mary an opportunity to look at her own behaviour and communication style when she is with certain individuals. Now that Mary has completed the tables, she can make some realistic decisions about with whom she will and will not communicate. As well she can make some decisions around her own behaviour when in the company of these individuals. Earlier I mentioned a very important concept in communicating effectively is the word *choice*.

First, let's look at Mary's feelings when she is communicating with her sister. She states she generally feels angry, betrayed, barely liked, and annoyed because her sister likes to pick fights, make rude comments, acts like a snob, and lies. Mary indicates that when around her sister, she behaves in a standoffish, aloof fashion. It sounds like Mary is not being her *authentic* self when around her sister. However, Mary does have some choices here. She can choose not to be around her sister; she can choose to tell her sister how her sister's behaviour affects her and request a change, or she can laugh at her sister's behaviour and take it with a grain of salt. After all, who wants to lose sleep over someone who behaves like your enemy?

Now, let's compare this to Mary's feeling when she is communicating with her boss. She states she generally feels angry and frustrated because he is dictatorial, patronizing, and doesn't listen to anyone's opinions but his own. Mary indicates when around her boss, she is shy, scared, apprehensive, and withdrawn. Again, let's look at Mary's choices. If Mary is going to be true to her authentic self, she can meet with her boss and express her thoughts and feelings. If she is not comfortable with a personal exchange, she can write her boss a note. Mary can involve the company's human resource department or employee assistance program for support. Mary can also choose to keep communication with her boss to a minimum. She can also look for another job.

Although each of these cases is different, it is easy to see that Mary does have some choice around how she will communicate with these two people. The goal of this exercise is to assist you, like Mary, to determine with whom you feel least comfortable communicating, why this is so, and how to change your behaviour and improve communication.

Now it's your turn.

Chapter Five | The Who and Why of Communication

Significant People With Whom You Communicate

Person	Rating (1-10)	1st thoughts I get when communicating	Feeling(s) I get when I communicate with this person	Why I get these feelings

Significant People With Whom You Communicate

Person	Rating (1-10)	1st thoughts I get when communicating	Feeling(s) I get when I communicate with this person	Why I get these feelings

Chapter Five | The Who and Why of Communication

Significant People With Whom You Communicate

Person	Rating (1-10)	1st thoughts I get when communicating	Feeling(s) I get when I communicate with this person	Why I get these feelings

Significant People With Whom You Communicate

Person	Rating (1-10)	1st thoughts I get when communicating	Feeling(s) I get when I communicate with this person	Why I get these feelings

Your Resulting Behaviour

People with Whom I Do Not Feel Comfortable Communicating	My Behaviour When I Am With This Person

What lessons did you learn from this exercise?

_____
_____
_____
_____
_____
_____
_____
_____

👉 Points to Remember From Chapter Five

- There are some people in our lives with whom we feel less comfortable communicating. There are a number of reasons why this is so. It is important for you to understand why you feel less comfortable speaking with some people and not others.

- A useful exercise is to use the chart provided and list the people with whom you communicate along with the associated thoughts and feelings you have while communicating.

- Notice the different thoughts and feelings you have and different behaviours you adopt with each person.

- This exercise lets you can examine both your communication style and associated behaviours.

- If you discover you feel more uncomfortable with some people than others, you can look at changing *your* behaviours when engaged with those whom you feel less comfortable.

- Once you understand your communication style and behaviours, the concept of *choice* can be applied. You can *choose* if you will communicate at all, and if so, choose how you will communicate and behave.

- The best rule of thumb is to be your authentic self in all situations. Only then will you be able to handle anything that comes your way.

Chapter Five | The Who and Why of Communication

What Have I Learned From This Chapter That Applies to Me?

What Will I Begin To Do Differently?

Chapter Six
The What and Where of Communication

It is pretty easy to identify **what** we don't like to communicate about. Develop your own list. My list would include things like, my mistakes, other people's mistakes, people and events that have made me sad, issues which may result in confrontation or disagreement and topics which may upset the listener(s).

How do we deal with these important issues? One rule of thumb includes sticking to the facts and saying what you have to say in as few words as possible. As I have said, anyone can say anything in five minutes or less. Practice what you are going to say in a mirror or role-play with a friend, stay in your adult *ego state*, don't get caught up in someone else's contrary attitudes, know when to remove yourself, don't repeat yourself, and make sure your body language is open and friendly.

Another skill I teach clients when speaking with someone about something difficult is to use the words *I* and *me*, and not the word *you*. When using *I* and *me*, you are taking responsibility for your own thoughts and not blaming someone else. Blaming only puts the listener on the defensive, which sabotages any prospect of a positive exchange.

For example, when talking to someone about a behaviour which upset you, say something like this: "*I* would like to speak with you about something that happened yesterday which upset *me*. *I* didn't appreciate it when confidential information about me was disclosed to Ralph. In the future, please don't divulge information of that nature without *my* consent."

The wrong way of saying this would look like this: "Yesterday, *you* disclosed confidential information about me to Ralph. *You* shouldn't have said anything. *You* were really out of line. Don't *you* ever do that again without my consent. What *you* did really bothered me."

Another important rule of thumb is to express both what you are *thinking* and *feeling*. You are made up of two very important parts, your ability to think and your ability to feel. When something happens, you have a cognitive (thought) experience and you have an emotional experience. If someone does something upsetting to you, your brain sends you a message, and so does your heart. When you respond to the person you have a responsibility to let them know how their actions affected you completely. For example, "*I* would like to speak with you about something that happened yesterday that upset *me*. *I* didn't appreciate it when confidential information about me was disclosed to Ralph. In the future, please don't divulge information of that nature without *my* consent. When I learned what had happened, I questioned our level of trust. I thought we had agreed on a protocol. Now this has happened, I feel very let down."

Teaching people how to express themselves from their "thinking self" and "feeling self" is very effective, particularly in family counselling. So often family members are unaware of how their actions affect those around them. We often make assumptions about issues and events only to find we were entirely wrong. However, by having someone tell us exactly how our behaviour affected them, we become enlightened about ourselves and can modify or change our actions in the future.

The Case of Lydia and Her Parents

I was seeing a mom, dad, and daughter about four years ago. The parents and sixteen-year-old Lydia had not been getting along for about one year. One issue Lydia had with her parents was their refusal to buy her a cell phone. Additionally, she complained Mom and Dad didn't always make note of her telephone messages. The parents justified their actions by saying a cell phone was too expensive, and the act of taking all of Lydia's phone messages was just too time-consuming. They couldn't understand why Lydia was getting so upset given she saw her friends daily and would be able to catch up on news then. Lydia and I practiced role-playing. She was then able to crystallize exactly how her parents' actions affected her. Lydia's presentation to her parents went like this: "It is very important to me that I receive all my telephone messages. If I put a writing pad by the phone with a pen, I would appreciate it if you could just take down the person's name and number. I don't expect you to take the message. I will ask my friends to monitor the number of calls they make to the house and explain how disruptive it is to you. When you refuse to take down my messages, I think you are mad at me or punishing me. I also think your refusal to take my messages is a bit mean and controlling. I always try to make sure I give you your messages. When I think you are mad at me, it frightens me because I don't know what I've done. I feel very sad and lonely to think you are purposely trying to be mean to me. I don't feel loved by you when things like that happen. I would like to talk with you about how we can resolve this."

When Lydia presented this to her parents at session, they were shocked to think Lydia thought they were mad and trying to punish her. They were even more taken aback to hear Lydia felt sad, lonely, and unloved. By expressing how she both thought and felt over a specific incident, Lydia and her parents were able to explore deeper issues in counselling and began to mend their relationship.

Couples who are having communication problems find it very helpful to learn the "think and feel" method of communication. Couples often assume they know what the other person is thinking or feeling. They are usually wrong.

The Case of Moe and Jane

Moe and Jane were seeing me for couple counselling. Jane believed Moe didn't help out enough with the household chores and child rearing. She always felt tired and haggard and like the *bad guy* around the children because she was the one doing the disciplining. She had a difficult time talking to Moe about this. He would become curt and dismissive, which only angered her. We worked together to help Jane and Moe talk this out. It went something like this:

JANE. Moe, I need your help with the housework and looking

after the kids. I don't have enough time in the day to look after all the chores and attend to the children's needs as well. By the end of the day, I'm really beat. Not only that, I think the children would also benefit by having you more involved.

MOE. I think I do my fair share around the house, and I try to spend as much time with the children as I can considering my schedule. I always free myself up for them on the weekend.

JANE. I know we both have very busy schedules, Moe, but I would like to do a better job at balancing our mutual responsibilities. When I don't get the support I need from you, I think I am a one-person band having to do all the work and make all the decisions. When I think like that, I feel very alone. Additionally, I feel terrible always playing the *bad guy* to the children because I am the only one who disciplines them. I need your help and involvement, and the children need your guidance. Besides, I miss you. I need us to work more like partners, more like we are on the same team. I have a few suggestions on how things can work a little more smoothly. I'm interested in what suggestions you have too. When do you think you would have a couple of minutes to talk?

You will notice Jane's use of *I* words. She didn't get caught up pointing her finger at Moe. She expressed what she thought and felt clearly and let Moe know what her expectations were. Additionally, she let Moe know she had some possible solutions to the problem and was interested in hearing his ideas as well. Jane made it clear she didn't want to corner Moe into a discussion but asked him when he could free himself up to talk; in other words, she left him wiggle room. It's important to give people time to digest what you have said particularly if you are looking for a response from them. Remember, you communicate from two places—think and feel. Let them be known!

Now we have talked about how to say the *what* part, we can move onto the *where* of communication. *Where* is perhaps the most important variable. The last place on earth you want to communicate about something important is in the wrong place. Have you ever been witness to a child having a temper tantrum in the middle of the grocery store? Arms waving like a windmill gone wild, feet kicking, screeching whales of protest, sobs of sadness? What a scene for a parent to deal with and in broad view of strangers, no less. It would be so much easier for the parent to deal with this scene in his or her home rather than in the middle of the produce aisle at the local groceteria.

"I always seem to blurt things out at the wrong place. It's so embarrassing," says a twenty-one-year-old client. "Last week I was in the women's washroom and said to my girlfriend, 'I wish my boss would stop checking up on everything I do. It drives me crazy. If she would just get a life, she wouldn't have to keep bugging me.'" As it turned out, her boss was in the next cubicle.

Another client recalls the story where she and her husband, with whom she worked, had been having marital problems for several months. Jennifer, who was still reeling from an argument the night before, blasted into the board room where her husband was meeting with a client. She became a human tornado as a blast of expletives landed on him like an unexpected avalanche.

Tony, upon learning his job was threatened, returned home to confide and find comfort in his wife, Liz, who was busy struggling to feed a precocious two-year-old and administer to a newborn infant with a fever. Tony plunked down at the table and began to vent enthusiastically. Liz attempted to digest what he was saying but was unable to listen attentively due to the children. Tony stormed from the room yelling, "If you don't give a damn, just say so. I don't appreciate being ignored!"

While on the telephone, a mom is approached by an excited fourteen-year-old, saying, "Mom, Mom, I need some money. Shelley's dad has offered to take us to the show, but it starts in fifteen minutes. We have to leave now. You have to get off of the phone and help me!"

Tracy, wanting to speak to her husband about her financial problems, chooses to speak with him over dinner. She prepares his favourite meal; sets the table with china, crystal, and candlelight; and chills the wine. Just as Jack is savoring the crispness of the wine, Tracy says, "Jack, I don't really know how to tell you this, but I invested all my inheritance in a company which just went bankrupt. I know we were planning on using that money for the new addition to the house. I'm really sorry."

Martha is hospitalized for breast cancer surgery. While she is in recovery, she asks for her husband. He is not to be found. When he arrives much later, he informs Martha that he will not be living in the house when she is released from hospital. He is leaving her for another woman.

All these incidents are true and did not have to unfold in the manner in which they did. Yes, communication is important, but picking the right time and place is vital to the outcome. Earlier we spoke about the word *responsibility*, the *ability* to *respond*. It is just as important to understand the ability to *present*.

Young children don't know any better. They tend to swarm their parents at the front door upon their return from work. They are excited to see Mom or Dad, and have many wonderful stories to share. Parents, however, are usually too exhausted at that very moment to appreciate their enthusiasm and need to catch their breaths and switch gears before settling into family dialogue. Adults, however, should know when it is and is not a good time to speak with someone. A good guide is to put yourself in the other person's shoes. If you are approaching someone about a private matter, you want to do so privately and not amidst other listening ears. Always exercise sensitivity and discretion.

👉 Points to Remember From Chapter Six

- When communicating, stick to the facts, say as few words as possible, don't repeat yourself, stay in your *adult ego state*, and don't get caught up in someone else's contrary attitudes.

- Know when to remove yourself.

- Keep your body language friendly and open.

- If necessary, practice what you are going to say in a mirror or role-play with a friend.

- Use the words *I* and *me*. Don't blame others.

- Take responsibility for what you *think* and *feel* and express it.

- Choosing *where* you communicate is vitally important. Also, know when it is and is not a good time to communicate.

- A good rule of thumb is to put yourself in the other person's shoes. Is this the right place?

- Keep private matters private.

What Have I Learned From This Chapter That Applies to Me?

Chapter Six | The What and Where of Communication

What Will I Begin To Do Differently?

Chapter Seven
The When of Communication

I go back to what I said earlier about being able to say anything to anyone in five minutes or less. You don't have to look for a long stretch of available time to say what you have to say to someone. However, the same rule of thumb applies as it did to the where of communication. Put yourself in the other person's shoes. If you are tired or not feeling well, you don't want to handle something requiring a lot of brain power. If you are in a rush, you don't want to be stopped and interrupted. If you are really enjoying yourself, you don't want to be struck with a piece of bad news.

Also, keep in mind if you are looking for a response from the other person, you may not get it right away. Earlier we said no response is a response. If someone is not giving you a response, a helpful thing to say is, "When would it be convenient for us to get together and talk about this?" or "Let's plan on talking about this later in the week when we both have had more time to think about it."

The time of day is also important when communicating. I have found you are more likely to have a successful exchange earlier in the day. Not so early that people are still sleepy but early enough to know people are awake and feeling fortified from breakfast. I also believe any time between 3:00 PM and

Chapter Seven | The When of Communication

dinner time is a less-than-desirable time to communicate about important matters. During this period your blood sugar level often drops, and you would often rather be snacking or napping. I like to chat about matters right after dinner, once the dishes are cleared away and people are feeling satisfied after a good meal. Work toward finding your own best time. And last, alcohol should always be avoided if you are planning to have an important talk with someone. Conversely, if the other person has been drinking, do not engage.

The When of Communication | Chapter Seven

☛ Points to Remember From Chapter Seven

- You can say anything to anyone in less than five minutes.

- Put yourself in the other person's shoes and try and understand where they are coming from before you approach them.

- If you don't want to discuss something, ask to defer the conversation.

- If you are looking for a response from someone, it is to your advantage to approach them at the most suitable time possible.

- It is also appropriate not to expect a response but to mutually agree on a time to revisit the issue and continue the conversation

- Again, put yourself in their shoes. Is this the right time to be communicating about this?

- Never begin an important conversation with someone if you or they, or you have been drinking.

What Have I Learned From This Chapter That Applies to Me?

What Will I Begin To Do Differently?

Chapter Eight
Pattern Interrupt

One of the most useful concepts I have taught to clients is the *pattern interrupt*. I began demonstrating the concept while giving seminars for the Canadian Mental Health Association about eighteen years ago. The association puts on a series of seminars for those who are recently separated. I present on "Effective Communications with Your Ex" on or around the fifth week of the series. Everyone files in as usual and takes their seats. After the program coordinator introduces me, I say hello to the group, and then I ask everyone to get up and find another seat. I ask no-one sit within four seats of someone they have previously sat beside. The group is always reluctant. I usually have to repeat the request and on one occasion had to physically help an individual get up from their seat while encouraging them to find a new location.

I am demonstrating that people do not like change. People don't even like to change where they have been sitting if they are familiar with the location and people with whom they have been sitting. I physically demonstrate the concept of interrupting an old pattern of behaviour, for example, sitting in the same location week after week, and replacing it with a new behaviour, moving to a new location surrounded by people with whom you are not familiar.

Pattern Interrupt | Chapter Eight

People rarely like to change anything they have become accustomed to, even if what they are accustomed to is not good for them. If you only pick up one glimmer of knowledge from reading this book, please let the *pattern interrupt* be the one thing you remember. Take a look at your life and look for reoccurring patterns of behaviour. For example, you have a boss who sits in his/her office and yells out to you in the reception area instead of getting up and speaking to you properly. Your past behaviour would have been to get up and go to her office to see what she wanted, thereby reinforcing the behaviour of being yelled at. A successful *pattern interrupt* would mean doing the opposite of what you previously did. You would *not* get up from your desk the next time your boss yelled out at you. After yelling out to you a few more times and not getting an answer, your boss will be compelled to get up and come out to you. When asked if you didn't hear being yelled at, you can reply with something like, "Instead of yelling out to me, it would be so much nicer if you could buzz me by phone or speak to me face-to-face. I'd like you to try this new approach."

🔍 The Case of Patty and John

Patty and John came for communications skills training noting Patty tended to be somewhat negative and always saw the glass half empty instead of half full. She would embellish the smallest of issues and build them into melodramas. She could never see the bright or funny side of things although she herself had a good sense of humour. The three of us agreed when John's wife next approached him with a tale of woe, he would respond with a burst of laughter. We agreed to this on the understanding that this action was not intended to belittle her but was an exercise intended to stop Patty's pattern of complaining and John's pattern of sympathizing.

On the couple's return visit the following week, the couple reported the following event. While walking the dog, Patty came across a group of youngsters on skateboards. They were doing risky stunts and making quite a lot of noise, which Patty found quite upsetting. The dog, on the other hand, thought the youngsters wanted to play and became quite excited. The added excitement of the dog heightened Patty's sense of anxiety. Patty became quite flustered and hurried home. Upon her return home,

Chapter Eight | Pattern Interrupt

Patty approached John in a flustered state, complaining about how poorly disciplined children are, the risks of skateboarding, and how she or the dog could have been seriously injured or killed.

As per our agreement, John responded with a burst of laughter. Initially Patty was slightly taken aback by this change. She wanted her husband to support her drama. However, her husband's laughter enabled her to see her story was not as dark and as terrible as she believed it to be at the time. She was even able to see the humourous side to her exaggerations. She was able to develop a healthy balance between reality and how she chose to perceive events.

The same week, Patty was busy in the kitchen preparing a meal for her sister's birthday. Instead of adding one-fourth teaspoon cayenne pepper, she added one and one-fourth teaspoons. She was horrified and let out a terrible squeal which John heard from the garage. He ran into the house thinking Patty had been seriously injured. He found her in tears over the stove. At first, he thought she had burned herself. When she described what had happened, John, right on cue, burst into laughter. Patty's first reaction was to throw something at him; she was so upset with his laughter. But at last, she started to laugh too and quickly changed the recipe into a Cajun masterpiece.

Another good example of the benefits of pattern interrupt refers to moms and dads who like to rescue their children. Parents sometimes believe they need to overcompensate for some reason, and hence, become overprotective. I'm sure their children do not appreciate this, especially as they grow older. An overly doting parent can diminish a child's sense of accomplishment. Eventually, and with help, these moms and dads can learn to use a *pattern interrupt* to change their own behaviour. As children face challenges, parents should support their decisions and actions as opposed to doing the deciding and taking the action for them. Parents need to learn to replace overprotective behaviour with encouraging actions like saying, "I'm sure you will work this out. You have dealt with similar things like this before. Just give it a little more thought. Let me know how it works out, or if there is anything I can do to help you." Remember to catch yourself because it is easy to fall back into old patterns.

Examine your own relationships and look for opportunities to interrupt old patterns of unhealthy behaviour and replace them with new ones. To begin, sometimes it's just easier to do the opposite of what you would have ordinarily done. At first, this may appear to be quite unusual. That's good. It means you are recognizing the change. The more you practice, the better you will become.

Chapter Eight | Pattern Interrupt

👉 Points to Remember From Chapter Eight

- *Pattern interrupt* means changing old *patterns* of behaviour into new behaviours.

- Generally, people do not like change even if what they are doing is not good for them.

- Try thinking of reoccurring *patterns* of behaviour you would like to *interrupt*. Initially, doing a pattern interrupt may mean doing the opposite of what you have been doing in the past. For example, if you have been phoning your child every day since he left home to attend university, *stop* phoning every day. Show him you trust and believe in his ability to look after himself.

What Have I Learned From This Chapter That Applies to Me?

Chapter Eight | Pattern Interrupt

What Will I Begin To Do Differently?

Chapter Nine
Be Proactive, Not Reactive

In this section I am going to help you recognize reactive communication and recommend how you can change this to proactive communication. Have you ever heard the saying "It's better to do it first rather than letting someone do it to you "? My children's phrase goes something like this, "You snooze, you lose." In other words, if you are going to be number one, you must act like number one. It means being your authentic self, taking responsibility and taking action.

Sit in the middle of the road long enough, and someone is sure to drive by and hit you. This behaviour is not being proactive. Proactive behaviour involves keeping off the street in the first place. Reactive behaviour is scampering to find safety upon hearing the sound of an oncoming vehicle.

Some synonyms for the word *active* include the following: *energetic, lively, caught up, embroiled, changing, participating, high power, kinetic, self-propelling,* and *vigorous*. What a marvelous selection of to-do words.

In order to be a proactive communicator, you have to be a *doer*. Many clients complain about a myriad of dreadful things that have happened to them. The truth, however, is people can be their own worst enemies. We are usually the cause of our own grief. Most personal problems stem from unresolved issues which people would rather blame on external events or others. It is much easier to think the cause of your problem is the result of something or someone else. *It's time to get out of the blame game!*

When young, we sometimes look for scapegoats to blame when we have done something wrong. Maturity should help us leave this behaviour behind. However, this is not always the case. I can't count the number of times I have heard statements like, "If it weren't for my teacher being so picky, I'd be getting great marks," "If it weren't for my bossy older brother, I'd be allowed to get my parent's car on the weekend," "If it weren't for my alcoholic husband, I'd be able to get a job I really like," "If it weren't for my stern mom, I'd be able to come and go as I pleased instead of living in this jail," "If it weren't for my wife being a workaholic, I would be able to enjoy a social life," "If it weren't for my children, I would be able to take extracurricular interest courses," and so on.

When you look at these scenarios realistically, there is very little one can do to change a picky teacher, bossy older brother, alcoholic husband, stern mom, workaholic wife, or the fact that one has children. However, there is something you can do about yourself. You can decide to respond to these situations pro-actively by asking yourself how *you* are contributing to these events and what *you* can do to change things. For example, the student who is getting poor grades would be better off asking herself the following questions:

- Do I attend all of my classes?

- Do I take good class notes?

- Do I spend enough time each day reviewing my class notes?

- Do I understand everything the teacher is talking about, and if not, do I ask questions?

- Do I make good study notes?

- Do I spend enough time studying for quizzes and exams?

Now let's look at the scenario where the younger brother blames his "bossy" older brother for not being able to use his parents' car on the weekend. In this case, the younger brother should be asking himself the following questions:

- Have I made a point of speaking with my parents regarding my thoughts and feelings?

- Have I done something to give my parents the impression I should not have the car on the weekends? If so, how can I remedy that impression?

- What can I do to improve my chances of being successful in getting the car for the weekend?

- If my brother needs the car for a good reason, what plans can I make to ensure I, too, have transportation over the weekend?

Now let's take a look at the interpersonal problem between the workaholic wife and husband who claims to have no social life. In this scenario, the husband should be asking himself the following:

- Have I made a point to speak with my wife regarding my thoughts and feelings?

- Do I do something to keep my wife from enjoying my company? What can I do to interest my wife in exploring a more active social life with me?

- If my wife is unable to reduce the time she works, what can I do to become more involved with my friends, family, and community?

- Why do I think it is my wife's responsibility to ensure I have an active social life?

You can see from these examples how easy it is to mistakenly blame an internal conflict on an external cause. When, in actual fact, the environment merely sets the stage for the internal conflict to be played out. When someone says, "My husband and I were so happy until he started his new job," the truth, more likely, is there were underlying tensions in the marriage before the husband got the new job. The stress or the changes resulting from the new job unleashed the preexisting problems in the marriage. The proactive response would be, "I recognize my husband and I are having some problems. It really came to light when he started his new job, and we had difficulty adjusting to the change." A proactive statement is a precursor to changing the situation. The change in this case is not to change the environment (the new job) but to change the marital relationship.

Often, I have seen couples for marriage counselling who have just bought a new house, just had a baby, or done both. Instead of dealing with internal conflicts within the marriage, the couple decides a change in their physical or family environment will remedy the problems. The couple then ends up with the added responsibility and stress of a mortgage or a new family member.

The exception however, is when a change in the environment will result in a healthier individual, for example, leaving an abusive relationship. An abused partner should always leave the relationship.

🔍 The Case of Rhonda

Rhonda came for counselling with a goal to improve her marriage to Don. She had been married for seven years. Prior to meeting her husband, she was a successful real estate agent. In fact, she met her husband through business. Don was an agent working in his father's company.

After marrying, Rhonda left her firm to join her father-in-law's company. It made good business sense, as it would increase her commission on sales, give Don and her an opportunity to help each other, and would result in greater flexibility around work schedules once children began to arrive.

Our first interview quickly revealed Rhonda felt trapped in her marriage and job. No children had arrived; her father-in-law had semi retired, leaving controllership of the business to Don; she rarely saw her husband given he was responsible for running the business; and Rhonda was exhausted having been given greater responsibility for sales and marketing.

What she had expected in her marriage and work had clearly not unfolded in its intended manner.

When I questioned Rhonda about leaving the company and working for someone else, she flatly refused claiming that leaving was not an option. She saw herself as indispensable and thought it would look poorly if she was to leave the family business. Despite the fact Rhonda disliked the added responsibility she had, disliked seeing her husband less often, and was heartbroken there didn't seem to be time to start a family, Rhonda did not want to take action to change her circumstances.

Rhonda was choosing to be reactive. She would rather blame her situation on things going on around her than look inwardly and examine decisions and choices she had made which contributed to her circumstance.

Through therapy, Rhonda was able to learn what the concepts of proactive behaviour and proactive communication meant. To begin, I asked Rhonda to list her goals. They included having children, working part-time, spending meaningful time with her husband, and finding time to spend with her friends and family.

After listing her goals, I asked Rhonda to list actions she would have to take to achieve these goals. First on the list was to improve her relationship, through improved communication, with Don. At the time Rhonda had been quarreling with Don quite a bit because she saw him as the cause of all *her* problems. Rhonda realized if she solved her own problems through proactive behaviour and talking with Don about her thoughts and feelings, she would stop making Don her enemy. She committed to speaking with Don about her personal goals and how he could assist her in achieving them. For example, Rhonda wanted Don to bring in more agents to help her out in the sales department. By doing this, Rhonda would have more time for herself and would feel emotionally and physically better. Rhonda also wanted to speak to Don about working toward starting their family. They had never really talked about it seriously because running the family business always took priority.

Through counselling Rhonda discovered she had always lived her life in reactive mode but learned she could take proactive steps to improve her personal and professional life.

Internal conflicts as described in "The Case of Rhonda" generally arise from a poor self-concept or weak ego strengths, and I refer the reader back to chapter 3, "Why Positive Self-Esteem Is Essential to Effective Communication." Reactive communication results when inner conflict spills out into the

Chapter Nine | Be Proactive, Not Reactive

environment, making the environment the enemy instead of acknowledging the inner conflict and addressing it.

Proactive communication gives you an opportunity to deal head-on with your reality. In other words, it gives you an opportunity to see yourself as you truly are and see others as they truly are as well. Proactive communication means you *do not* blame, whine, scheme, or avoid.

Blaming helps you to avoid acknowledging your participation in a problem. In most problem situations, one individual is rarely the problem. There are usually a few contributors. It takes two to tango. The most gratifying moment for me is when a client can persuade their mate to join them in couple counselling. So often I hear wives say, "My husband is paying to send me here to get fixed." A proactive communicator, on the other hand, will admit their participation in the problem and avoid blaming either themselves or the other, but commit to participating in the solution.

Whining protects you from being confronted. It is difficult to bring reality to one's attention if they are playing the helpless victim. I had a client who said he could not work again because he could not get over his wife leaving and subsequently divorcing him. He couldn't make any decisions about his life or his future at large. He chose to wallow in self-pity and was also able to recount several stories confirming a history of helplessness. As far as he was concerned, it was his therapist's responsibility to figure his life out and tell him what to do. A proactive communicator would approach this situation by saying something like, "I am recently divorced and having a difficult time getting over it. I feel almost paralyzed and would like some guidance about what I can do to move forward."

Another helpless communicator is the *confused* individual: "I am so confused I don't know what to do," "I'm so confused I don't understand what the problem is," "When you talk to me like that, I get so mixed up," "I can't handle all this information; it puts me on overload," and so on. Instead of being a proactive communicator and dealing with the issue, the individual hides behind a cloud of confusion. Life, in fact, is not confusing at all, however we can certainly take a good stab at making it so if it fits our needs.

Scheming is another reactive behaviour. It helps to hide you from reality. Schemers are so busy manipulating others by inventing rules and playing games they avoid the possibility of having to make a decision, thus thrusting the responsibility onto someone else. Schemers are also very seductive because they have had to master the art of persuasion.

Avoiders are very good at spending a lot of time living in the past and/or planning the future. They are able to live in the past because it is known and comfortable. Likewise, they can dream into the future because it is not yet real. As long as people live in the past or future, they never have to get to know themselves and experience new thoughts and feelings in the present. Who they were in the past is now gone and who they are to be in the future has yet to happen. I have a friend who once told me if you stand with one foot behind you planted in the past and one foot in front of you planted in the future, you will pee on the present. Try this, you will know what she is talking about.

Proactive communicators do not avoid but ask, "What am I thinking and feeling right now?" "What am I feeling toward you right know?" "Am I doing anything to sabotage this communication right now?" Proactive communication means living in the present and staying there.

If you can see yourself in any of the above examples, make a commitment to yourself today to change. Catalogue the number of times you blame your problems on someone or something else. Look for avoidance talk and scheming. Dare to know yourself and others. Become an active participant in your life and enjoy the thrill of putting your authentic signature on everything you say and do. You are totally unique and unlike anyone else in the world.

Setting your own goals is the key to being proactive. Some people like to make five-year life plans (or two years or three years and so on). By doing this, you are able to set out what you hope to achieve as well as the necessary corresponding actions required to succeed.

🔍 The Case of Molly

Following her separation in December 1980, Molly developed a five-year life plan. The plan had short-and long-term goals. Her short-term goals included establishing a budget and selling her marital home. After establishing her

Chapter Nine | Be Proactive, Not Reactive

budget, she discovered she didn't have enough money to live on; therefore, she started a part-time cottage industry making dough dolls, which are decorative wall ornaments made from bread dough. The money raised from her business was enough to cover the weekly grocery bill. She also ordered a cord of wood to heat her home with the fireplace in order to reduce her gas bill. All the while she continued to say to herself, "I *can* and I *will.*"

Knowing she wanted to continue working, she had to address the problem of no longer having a second income to cover day care costs (her children were four and one and a half years old at the time). The challenge was quickly remedied by offering free room and board and a fair salary to a kind, reliable young woman who had recently been kicked out of her parents' home. After all, with her husband gone, there was extra room in the house!

She knew she needed a lawyer but put that on hold pending the sale of her home. It finally did sell in the spring at which time she held a huge garage sale; the funds from which went toward the first and last months' rent on her new apartment, as no funds were realized from the sale of the house.

The next part of her plan was to move her family and babysitter from Burlington to Oakville into the apartment she was able to sublet from a friend who was moving. Having no money, she asked her friends to help her move. Thank God for good friends.

With the move from her home into an apartment, she finally had a little free cash each month and was able to hire a lawyer, develop a new budget which included saving to buy a home and some play money with which to entertain and treat her children. She also realized she needed to acquire a better-paying job in order to maintain a comfortable middle-class lifestyle for her girls.

Over time she realized her goals - returned to school part-time, got a divorce, and eventually moved her children into a home where they once again had a backyard to play in. Although her home was a handy man's special at the time of purchase, she and her friends laboured to turn it into a real gem. She did return to school part-time and upon graduation secured a position which virtually doubled her income overnight.

Her plan, positive attitude, open communication and emotional support from her children and friends provided a road map to the future. It gave her stability during a very rough time. It allowed her to behave and communicate pro-actively and design her own destiny. It gave her confidence in herself when she felt most vulnerable, and all the while her children continued to grow into the loving, beautiful people they are today.

Had she behaved and communicated reactively, she would have waited for the bank to foreclose on her house and been forced to leave her job and go on welfare in order to avoid paying exorbitant day care costs, which she could ill afford. She would have been unable to afford the tuition fee to return to school and would have had no career to return to once she no longer qualified for government subsidies. Her children would not have been able to participate in dance, music, and drama classes; would not have been able to go to their favourite summer camp; and would never have had a backyard to play in.

Like I said earlier, being proactive means having a purpose, thinking strategically to put yourself in situations which support your success, developing goals and action plans, and then sticking to your plan by being a determined communicator.

Behaving pro-actively is something you can incorporate into your everyday life by knowing how to communicate with yourself and others. To communicate pro-actively with yourself means asking yourself what is best for you and then setting out to achieve it. Communicating pro-actively with others means negotiating the best mortgage rate and day care fee. It means telling others you have parameters within which you work, live, and play and you would like them to be respected. When you communicate pro-actively, you are sending the message you believe in yourself and are in control of your future. Proactive words include *I can, I will, I like, I don't like, yes*, and *no*, to name a few. You will notice reactive people tend to use words like *maybe, we'll see, perhaps, sort of, kind of, I don't know, I'm not sure*, and *I can't*.

Take some time now and think about how you communicate with yourself and others. If you tend to be more reactive than proactive, begin today by incorporating more proactive words and actions into your vocabulary and life style. Remember, it's all right to take baby steps. Change takes place slowly. What is important is your will to change.

This is a good time to incorporate a mantra into your daily routine. You

Chapter Nine | Be Proactive, Not Reactive

will recall from Chapter 3, a *mantra* is a special message you say to yourself several times a day. The message you send yourself will eventually be picked up by your subconscious mind and will be translated into conscious actions.

Script a mantra which will tell your subconscious mind you are positive and proactive. A mantra could go something like this: "I, [insert first and last name], am in control of my destiny. I am self-directed. I think positively and behave pro-actively. To the best of my ability I will ensure successful outcomes in what I do." Remember, being proactive means thinking positively and planning purposely. My eldest daughter always encouraged her sister by reminding her of the story about the smallest train who was trying to climb the largest mountain. With each turn of its wheels, the train said, "Yes, I can. Yes, I can. Yes, I can . . ."

👉 Points to Remember From Chapter Nine

- People who live pro-actively strategically place themselves in environments which will support their ability to achieve, take responsibility for their actions, and don't blame others for negative outcomes.

- People who live reactively tend to blame their troubled circumstances on things which go on around them.

- People can become chronically reactive and completely abdicate responsibility for their actions thus blaming their failing life on people and events going on around them.

- Becoming proactive means looking inwardly and examining decisions and choices you have made.

- Developing a *life plan* can assist you I achieving your goals.

- It is important to communicate pro-actively with yourself as well as with others by using words like *I can, I will, I like, I don't like.*

- You can change your behaviour and communication from reactive to proactive by taking baby steps. Make small changes first. Small changes grow into large changes over time.

- Incorporating daily *mantras* and *positive self-talk* will assist you in becoming more proactive. Develop your own personal mantras.

- Being proactive means thinking positively and planning purposefully.

Chapter Nine | Be Proactive, Not Reactive

What Have I Learned From This Chapter That Applies to Me?

What Will I Begin To Do Differently?

Chapter Ten
Listen, Listen, Listen

Marketing experts tell us you have to tell people something eight times before they really hear what has been said. What a sorrowful state of affairs. No wonder advertising companies pay a fortune to develop ads and commercials to catch our attention.

Now, translate that knowledge into your daily communication with others. It is surprising we hear what anybody has to say. Why is this? I believe this is so because we have never been taught to listen. Long past are the days when children "were seen and not heard" (Personally, I do not agree with this concept). To the contrary, from a very young age, children are encouraged to talk, be the centre of attention, and engage in conversations with one and all. When siblings arrive, children then learn to outtalk or out volume one another. This is fine, but for the fact children are not taught to listen. If parents spent as much time teaching their children to listen as they do teaching their children to speak, I believe communications between people would improve immeasurably.

For a number of years I have had the opportunity to work with the Aboriginal people of Ontario. They have taught me many valuable lessons about communicating, some of which I have incorporated into my family counselling practice. Aboriginal people have taught me the skill of *listening*. When I speak of listening, I think of entering a forest and being able to hear a brook running downstream not far away, or hearing the echo of wind against leaves. It means being *focused*.

Aboriginal people have taught me the beauty of listening through what I call the "learning circle." The circle can be comprised of any number of people of all ages who sit side by each in a circle. A circle represents continuity and evolution. An elder will begin the circle with a blessing and by giving thanks to the Creator. The elder asks every participant to speak from a good and kind place from within their heart. There is no hierarchy within the circle. The status of all members is equal. The goal of the circle is to give everyone an opportunity to speak, uninterrupted and in their own time. The underpinnings of the circle are respect for self and others. After the blessing, the elder may begin the circle by telling a story or speaking to an issue which has personal importance or may sing a song. The point is to share your true self (your thoughts and feelings) with the group and know you are in safe company to do so. No one is permitted to interrupt the person who is speaking. Those remaining in the circle must listen and learn. When the elder is finished, he or she will pass the revered eagle feather or a carved talking stick onto the person sitting next to them. When you are in possession of the feather or stick, you can decide whether or not to speak. Whatever the case, when you have finished, you pass the stick along until everyone has had an opportunity to share a part of themselves with the group.

I was given a carved wooden talking stick by a very special friend. It is about seven inches long and carved from a beautiful soft wood. Grandfather sun has been meticulously carved on its face. The stick is well balanced and has the worn texture of something which has been touched by many hands.

I use the learning circle forum for family counselling, and I never cease to marvel at its success. To begin, it teaches us we would rather interrupt than listen. It teaches us that to hear is very easy but to listen is very complex. It teaches you must really *want* to listen to someone in order to really get to know who they are. It teaches us if you are really listening to someone, you

Chapter Ten | Listen, Listen, Listen

cannot be thinking about your reply. It teaches us in order to truly listen, you must put your own mind clutter on hold. It teaches that listening involves intuition as well. It teaches what we say may have several layers of meaning. It teaches us that speaking our thoughts and feelings out loud helps to clarify our confusion, and it teaches once you verbalize something, you must take ownership for it. It teaches respect for others.

I have read we speak, on average, over two hundred words per minute to say nothing of the nonverbal communication taking place simultaneously. If you take note of the length of time you usually speak to someone, you begin to understand the enormity of the task of real listening. If you begin to daydream for only a moment, valuable insight and information can be lost.

We must also not underestimate the value of nonverbal communication as it validates what the person is saying. If, for example, I have a client who is smiling while telling me about a recent tragedy, what the client is saying is incongruent with how he or she is feeling. Or, if I have a client who is looking remorseful while telling me they just bought their dream car, again what the client is saying is incongruent with how he or she is feeling. This incongruence will need clarification. True listening means being able to interpret the slant of the jaw, body posture, movement, tone and intonation of the voice, and the look in someone's eyes. Perhaps our eyes are the window of our souls. They can say anger, love, suspicion, confusion, boredom, and more all in a blink. True listening also means being able to interpret the sounds people make. My grandmother used to sigh heavily when she was feeling tired or stressed. My mother subsequently learned that behaviour. My daughter laughs when she is feeling nervous or anxious. When I am upset, I also breathe heavily. When I was in university, I had a friend who used to burp when he got nervous. Exam time was extremely difficult for him.

Listening also means being able to interpret another person's silence. I had a professor who once said "silence is golden". It gives the person an opportunity to reflect upon what they have just said. People often gain new insight by giving themselves the opportunity to silently reflect on new information. It is important not to interrupt that silence. Just don't confuse this with being *given* the silent treatment. The silent treatment has nothing to do with listening. This is when you say to yourself, "Whose problem is this?" and remove yourself from the situation.

A long time ago I befriended an elderly woman who has become incredibly special to me. As such, I have taken a great deal of time to learn what she is really saying to me when she speaks. For reasons unknown to me, she was trained by her parents never to communicate clearly or directly. Her thoughts may not have been received as valuable, or she may have been overshadowed by other siblings. I don't know. In any event, she learned to speak in a way which *hoped* the listener would figure out and understand what she was trying to say. Guess what? That rarely happened, and sadly she taught other family members to communicate just like her! Hoping others will decipher what you are really trying to say just isn't productive. To be honest, it is quite unfair to give the responsibility of figuring out what you are trying to say to the listener. For example, we were sitting out on the back deck one evening when she said to me, "Are you cold?" It was a warm evening, and I was a bit surprised she had asked. After giving it more thought, I returned the question and asked if she was cold. "Yes," she said. I was then able to offer to bring her a sweater. It would have made things so much easier if she had just told me she was cold and asked me to bring her a sweater.

This is a good example of someone having learned to ask questions to get out of ever having to make "I" statements and bear the responsibility for having done so. Another good example is asking, "What shall we have for dinner?" instead of saying, "I would like to have fish for dinner this evening." If people don't make statements, they are likely to end up getting spaghetti for dinner instead of fish.

Always be clear and direct when you speak and try to avoid asking questions. Make statements. Don't put the listener in the position of trying to figure out what you are saying. Chances are you will be blamed for not getting their message. Whose fault is that? Not yours.

If someone is not being clear and direct, tell them, and ask them to speak clearly. Insist on it. Do not take responsibility for someone else's inability to communicate well. Take responsibility for listening actively and requesting clarity in return.

👉 Points to Remember From Chapter Ten

- If you are a parent, please teach your children the importance of listening and, further, how to listen with their hearts.

- There is a large difference between hearing and listening. Hearing entails picking up on sounds. Listening entails understanding the meaning of what is being spoken and attending to nuances and body language. Learn to value nonverbal communication.

- Listening means being entirely focused. Get rid of the mind clutter.

- The goal of listening is to *understand* clearly what the person is trying to communicate. If you don't understand, seek clarification until you do understand. Do not be made the scapegoat because someone thought you understood.

- When you listen, you assume 100 percent responsibility of the communications process regardless of whether or not you agree with the speaker. Listening is selfless.

- Listen from a good place. Every one is an equal. There is no hierarchy. Create respect.

- Never interrupt unless the reason is to seek clarification.

- When listening properly, you are not formulating your response at the same time.

- Watch for nonverbal cues and listen to what people are not saying to you. Insist they be clear and direct especially where inconsistencies appear.

👉 Points to Remember From Chapter Ten

- Everyone present should be given an opportunity to share and listen in turn.

- Another role for the listener is to create an atmosphere of safety and acceptance.

- Listening also means being comfortable with silence.

Chapter Ten | Listen, Listen, Listen

What Have I Learned From This Chapter That Applies to Me?

What Will I Begin To Do Differently?

Chapter Eleven
Body Language

The better part of communication is body language. I have mentioned this earlier, but it is so important it is worth examining more fully.

Body language refers to how you hold your entire body, including head, arms, hands, legs, and feet. It also includes facial gestures. Earlier I said positive communication will result if you show respect and positive regard for the person with whom you are communicating. It is also necessary to show respect and positive regard through appropriate body language. You do this by physically attending to the communicator thereby showing what they have to say is important.

Body language also tells others how you feel about yourself. Do you recall Ellen from chapter 4 when in the company of her husband, hid herself behind crossed arms and legs and diminished her size by curling forward into a small ball?

Let's begin with some easy and simple rules. Always face the person with whom you are communicating. Look straight into their eyes (this is especially important for men). Make sure your face is saying, "I'm enjoying this conversation." Don't frown or purse your lips, squint or make question marks with your eyebrows. Don't look surprised at what the person is saying. Respect and positive regard are unconditional. Keep your head straight. A chin too high can be perceived as arrogance; a chin too low can be perceived as boredom.

Your back should be relaxed and support open arms. Hold your arms loosely at your sides or resting on armrests if sitting in a chair. Crossed arms send the message "I don't want you getting close to me." Hands should be relaxed with extended fingers. Clenched hands look like fists. Keep your fingers open and, if gesturing with your hands never, show the palm. The palm of the hand could easily spur a flashback of an unwanted slap by someone in their past. If you want to make a point, it is acceptable to bring your fingers together and, with the back of your hand toward the listener, make small hand gestures. *Never point*. Keep your hands within you own personal body space. One's personal body space is around eighteen inches from the body.

Legs should be relaxed. Crossing at the ankles is preferred over crossing at the knees. Or just plant your feet at shoulder-distance apart.

It is important to keep the body still. You can probably recall trying to speak with someone whose leg or foot kept tapping or jiggling, or someone who tapped their fingers on a table or countertop. Your message should say "calm" as opposed to "I can't wait until you're gone!"

Yawning at someone is a real *no-no*.

It is valuable for both men and woman to appreciate the impact of their body size. Since women are usually smaller, it is sometimes necessary for us to project ourselves as being larger. I had a client who was the only female teacher at a primary school. She was very petit, perhaps five feet tall, and weighted approximately one hundred pounds. She told me she felt quite intimidated at the weekly staff meetings. She could barely be seen at the board room table let alone be heard among the loud and overbearing presence of her male colleagues.

I suggested Danielle adopt some male mannerisms. I asked her to watch men's body language. Some men like to spread their bodies out. They raise their arms and place their hands behind their head, making the distance between their elbows about two and a half feet. This small gesture increases their size considerably. If this is done while standing, a formidable image is

Chapter Eleven | Body Language

created given men are generally taller than women.

While sitting, some men like to get comfortable by stretching their arms out on either side of them and resting their arms on the backs of chairs, even if you happen to be sitting in one. In addition, they may raise one leg up and place their ankle on the opposing knee. Nothing is wrong with these gestures but they due tend to give the impression of increased size. Men have to be sensitive to the impact their body size can have on women. Even though not intending to, a tall or large man can be easily perceived as towering over and breathing down on someone. Even the size of a man's foot can look intimidating if he's crossed his ankle over his knee and his size 14 shoe is inches from you. I know a young man who wears a size 14 shoe. He is as gentle as a lamb. However, when he is nervous or upset, he jiggles his feet back and forth or crosses his legs at the knee and kicks his foot out and back repeatedly. This behaviour is not conducive to focused communication.

At the next staff meeting Danielle sat erect in her chair, leaned back slightly, and placed her hands behind her head. I advised her to *mirror* the body language of her male colleagues. I also advised her to speak more slowly, to drop the pitch of her voice, and to speak louder than normal. She said it felt incredibly awkward initially, but it did bring some attention her way. She immediately looked larger and like more of an equal with her colleagues. She remarked her colleagues listened to her comments and appeared genuinely more attentive.

With each staff meeting, Danielle incorporated more mirroring behaviours. Increasingly she felt more comfortable with her colleagues and the manner in which they communicated together.

As noted, this simple technique is called "mirroring." It is very simple to learn. You just mirror the behaviours of the person with whom you are communicating. If they lean forward, you also lean forward. If they rest their chin in their hands, you do likewise. Studies show we are attracted to people who behave as we do.

Body Language | *Chapter Eleven*

Another important point around body language is respecting and keeping out of a person's personal space unless invited to go there. Likewise, if someone touches you and you would rather they not, tell them. Getting to know someone will give you the opportunity to learn how comfortable they feel about sharing their personal space. Also, be aware different cultures share different beliefs about personal space. This should always be respected.

Now we have discussed how our body language can impact others, let's talk about listening to our own bodies.

Your body will communicate with you and tell you how you are feeling long before your mind will. When I am feeling anxious or tense, my left shoulder creeps up toward my left earlobe. Inevitably I get a stiff neck and back. I also press my tongue against the roof of my mouth, resulting in a sore jaw and headache.

Learn how to listen to your body and do regular body checks. I suggest you put little stickers around places you most frequent - the telephone, the refrigerator, the bathroom, your office, and so on. Each time you see a sticker, take one minute to mentally scan down your body and look for signs of discomfort, stress, and tension. Begin with your head. Are your eyebrows relaxed or furrowed, are your teeth clenched together, or is your tongue pressed against the roof of your mouth? Are your lips pursed? Is your neck relaxed?

Move on to your shoulders, arms, and back. Are your shoulders down and back? Is your spine erect? Are the muscles in your back relaxed? Does your chest feel compressed? Is your breath slow and deep, or is it shallow? Does your stomach feel relaxed, tense, or upset? Do your arms fall by your sides comfortably? Are your hands unfolded or in a fist? Are your legs crossed or relaxed? Are your feet still? Do you have an overall sense of well-being?

Let your body communicate with you. Listen to its every signal. Do your body checks at least four times daily. If, while doing your body check, you find areas of stress, stop for a few moments and do some relaxation breathing. It is virtually impossible to hold stress while doing relaxation breathing. After doing three to four minutes of deep breathing, get on with your day.

Chapter Eleven | Body Language

The more you practice doing your body checks, the better you will become. Soon, you will not need to use stickers to remind yourself to do a body check. Your mind will know every time you look at your telephone, refrigerator, around your office, etc., you are to do a body check. It will become a habit.

It is also a good idea to get into the habit of doing relaxation breathing throughout the day just to feel better. It not only relaxes the mind and body but refreshes your oxygen supply by taking in and expelling deep belly breaths.

Relaxation Through Breathing

Breathing is the easiest way to relax. This is a simple exercise to calm your mind and body. Some people think you have to be a yoga practitioner or a student of spirituality to learn and practice relaxation breathing. This is absolutely not true. Everyone from children to elders can easily learn and practice this stress-reduction technique, and you can do it almost anywhere at any time.

The Technique I Suggest

Sit or lie down comfortably. I always suggest you put one hand on your heart (your love centre) and one hand on your diaphragm (your control centre). Hold yourself caringly and close your eyes.

First, take a big breath out through your mouth and consciously try to relax your body. Next, close your mouth and inhale through your nose slowly. Mentally count to four or five while breathing in if you can. Then hold that breath for a count of three to four. Initially, some people may feel faint doing this. If this happens, just hold that breath for a couple of seconds. Next, exhale through your open mouth slowly. You want to hear yourself blowing out. Note that exhaling takes longer than inhaling. When blowing out, you want to make sure you get all the excess air out of your lungs. Since most people pant and do not breathe properly, air that should have been expelled is often not. Be mindful of getting rid of this. This is the completion of one perfect relaxation breath.

You want to repeat his cycle as long as you feel comfortable. I suggest clients do their relaxation breathing at least four times a day for two to four minutes at a time. Some of the more practiced clients are able to do this for several minutes. Always do this breathing exercise when you go to bed to help you fall asleep.

The last thing to remember is to just listen to your body breathing. You don't have to imagine a picture or hum or repeat a word to induce a state of relaxation. All you have to do is concentrate on listening to yourself breath.

Please make sure you remember to do this when you are feeling particularly anxious, out of focus, or stressed. I have heard it said it is physically impossible to have an anxiety attack while doing relaxation breathing.

Points to Remember From Chapter Eleven

- A large part of communication is body language.

- Body language refers to how you hold your entire body while communicating. It also includes gestures and facial expressions.

- It is necessary to show respect and positive regard in your body language. You do this by physically attending to the person with whom you are communicating. For example, leaning forward, looking directly into their eyes, having a pleasant facial expression.

- Body language also communicates how you feel about yourself. For example, are you hiding behind crossed arms and legs, are you fidgeting, do you have a scornful expression?

- In general, your body should be relaxed and welcoming and say, "I am interested in what you have to say."

- Never point.

- Respect one's personal body space and don't let anyone invade yours without your permission.

- Be aware body size can communicate a message in itself.

- *Mirroring behaviour* is a simple technique which involves mirroring the mannerisms of the person with whom you are communicating.

- Different cultures have different norms around body language. Don't expect everyone to have the same customs as your own. Be respectful.

👉 Points to Remember From Chapter Eleven

- Never shy away from a handshake.

- It is also important to listen to your own body's language.

- Your body will often tell you how you are feeling long before your mind will.

- Doing regular *body checks* keeps us in touch with how we are feeling.

- Relaxation breathing should be done daily and included in your bedtime regime.

Chapter Eleven | Body Language

What Have I Learned From This Chapter That Applies to Me?

What Will I Begin To Do Differently?

Chapter Twelve
The Authentic Self

As we begin to develop personal and work relationships, we are compelled to decide how we want others to perceive us. For example, I want a potential friend to know who I really am, what I like and don't like, what I will and will not do, my values, and personal boundaries. I want them to know I place a high value on humour, independence, generosity, affection, compromise, honesty, straightforwardness, and fairness. I want them to know I dislike rudeness, cattiness, selfishness, self-centeredness, and people who use others. I want to ensure I represent myself clearly to others and live by my values and standards in all relationships. People who fail to do this suffer the loss of their *authentic self*.

Over many years I have witnessed hundreds of clients who no longer know their authentic self because they either gave it away or allowed it to be changed or taken by someone else.

🔍 The Case of Richard and Martin

Richard and Martin met at the local gym. Martin was seventeen years older than Richard. Over time they developed a caring relationship, which grew into romantic intimacy.

The Authentic Self | Chapter Twelve

Six months into the relationship, I received a phone call from Richard requesting an appointment.

Richard described his relationship with Martin as fun and adventurous. He respected and loved Martin and cherished Martin's family, who had accepted Richard immediately. He admired Martin's astute business sense and had successfully partnered with him on a few ventures. He enjoyed the financial stability resulting from them living together. Martin also recognized additional savings due to the shared expenses. Both Richard and Martin enjoyed entertaining, dining out, and traveling. They shared a mutual group of friends. All seemed well on the surface.

However, when I began to ask Richard about his true self, how he identified himself; in other words, about his *authentic self*, a different picture emerged. Richard liked quiet, intimate evenings with Martin. Martin always liked to be with friends. Richard wanted to spend more time with his family. Martin saw that as a waste of time. Richard liked a tidy apartment where Martin preferred Richard to pick up after him. Richard valued friendship with both gay and straight people whereas Martin rarely ventured outside the gay community. Richard was an amateur actor but felt compelled to give this up to support Martin's business interests and associates. This resulted in Richard missing his theater friends and missing auditions for new roles. Richard liked to restrict his caretaking to work where he practiced as a nurse whereas Martin wanted Richard to tend to his every scrape and bruise, which Richard gave into. Richard believed in a monogamous relationship where Martin mentally separated love from sex and believed having a few sexual partners was acceptable.

Richard was telling me he had not presented his authentic self to Martin from the outset and subsequently abandoned his core beliefs to satisfy Martin. Early in the relationship, Richard believed he could adjust to Martin's likes and dislikes and believed he could change Martin's thinking on a few issues (*which never happens*). Over time Richard discovered he was not being his authentic self in the relationship and found himself struggling to regain his belief system, those important qualities that defined who he was. He longed to live authentically once again.

Through therapy Richard was able to understand what had happened between Martin and him. He saw how he had, out of love, sacrificed his most

Chapter Twelve | The Authentic Self

integral qualities and beliefs - his *authentic self*. I encouraged Richard not to judge Martin but invite him to join in couple counselling, where each could help the other better understand their *authentic selves*. From there, they could decide if their relationship could continue.

Living your authentic self in a relationship will result in emotional intimacy between partners. Emotional intimacy results when behaviour and communication are transparent and both able to reveal there authentic selves (thoughts, feelings and behaviours) in an environment of unconditional love, trust and acceptance. Emotional intimacy is the all important glue that keeps relationships together.

🔍 The Case of Diana and Jay

Diana and Jay had been married for fourteen years. Two months before entering counselling, Diana discovered Jay was involved with another woman - a colleague in his office. The extramarital affair began eight months before Diana's discovery.

Diana was prepared to address the issues that came between them if Jay was willing to say good-bye to his affair with Jodi. From the time Diana learned of her husband's affair, Jay kept moving between the two women. At one moment he would say he didn't love Jodi anymore and committed to his marriage. However, a few weeks later, Jay would fall into a depression and run back to Jodi. This scenario lasted two months until Diana finally persuaded Jay to begin marriage counselling.

Therapy allowed them to learn how both had adopted distancing behaviours over the years resulting in Jay falling out of love with Diana. Their marriage became a partnership of convenience and safe predictability for Jay. The relationship was "easy." He loved Diana, but he loved her like you would a lifelong friend. His love no longer filled him with romantic intrigue, excitement, emotional intimacy, and sexual desire. Thus, Jay sought emotional and sexual intimacy elsewhere.

Diana, on the other hand, was committed to her husband and wanted the marriage to work, which is why Jay had agreed to counselling. It also appeased his overwhelming sense of guilt.

The Authentic Self | Chapter Twelve

During our sessions together, we talked about the *authentic self*. They were both able to communicate the difference between the "self" which entered the marriage fourteen years ago and the "self" which remained now. Diana admitted that at times she didn't like who she became when she was with Jay. She remembers herself being much more fun to be with. She liked to have fun, laugh, and be spontaneous. However, she indicated "Jay's moodiness" over the years made her more somber. At times she felt as if she had to "walk on eggs."

She didn't enjoy her sexual self either. She always instigated making love with Jay, and at times she felt Jay recoiled from her touch. Having recently learned of Jay's affair, she couldn't imagine him behaving in such an icy manner with Jodi.

After four counselling sessions, Diana phoned to set an appointment. Jay had left her for Jodi leaving behind a note which read something like this:

Dear Diana,

I can't continue treating you like this. It isn't fair to either of us. I will always be grateful for the time we had together, but I now realize I can't continue being someone I'm really not in our marriage. Sometimes I even wonder who I really am. I know this must sound confusing, but somewhere along the way I stopped being my authentic self. Perhaps I thought I'd find it with Jodi. Maybe that's wrong. I'm not sure of a lot of things right now. But I do know that I have to regain a sense of who I am, where I'm going, and how I am going to get there. I will not run back into your life again giving us both a sense of false hope. It's time for me to move on.

Jay

Inasmuch as Diana was distraught over the termination of their marriage, she knew she didn't want Jay bouncing in and out of her life. At the same time, she was able to begin looking into the future and setting some personal goals. Diana stayed in counselling throughout the separation.

Chapter Twelve | The Authentic Self

Over the next few months, Diana and Jay sold their home. With the money realized from the sale, Diana was able to purchase a smaller home in another city, which was closer to her family and friends. She joined a support group for the newly separated and began taking yoga classes. She also joined the local fitness club. Life was looking better.

The *authentic self* means you are living who you really are to yourself and to others. It means loving yourself unconditionally to enable you to speak the truth, validate your thoughts and feelings, and support others to do the same. We all know right from wrong and what we like and dislike, but even so, many continue to sacrifice or ignore personal needs for the sake of someone else. In doing this, our subconscious mind is constantly sent the message "You are not good enough; it's okay for you to come second or third or last. Your needs are less important than everyone else's."

Being authentic is being genuine. Genuineness is born from a beautiful place within. It is humble, loving, generous, and forgiving. It looks to the win-win in all situations. It does not sacrifice, and it does not expect others to sacrifice. It is good, just like you.

Points to Remember From Chapter Twelve

- The *authentic self* is the person you truly are to yourself. It is what you like and don't like, your values and belief system, and your standards. It is the *honest* you without pretense. It means loving yourself unconditionally to enable you to speak the truth, validate your thoughts and feelings, and support others to do the same.

- Sometimes when we are involved in a relationship, we can lose our authentic self because we voluntarily give it away, or we allow it to be taken from us.

- When you lose your *authentic self*, you lose the definition of who you really are. It is not uncommon for people to arrive for counselling saying, "I don't know who I am anymore."

- If this happens, it is important to begin redefining yourself via your core belief system and values and decide what you want for yourself regardless of others around you.

- Once you have redefined your *authentic self*, it is then possible to move forward within your own framework of who you really are and make appropriate life choices.

- There are really six people operating in every relationship. Who I really am, who I project I am, and who you think I am. The same goes for the other person. Therefore, you must present your authentic self to ensure greater emotional intimacy with your partner. Emotional intimacy will then translate into unconditional love and acceptance of yourself and partner and a strengthened commitment to your journey together.

- The goal is emotional intimacy gained by exposing your innermost thoughts and feelings. By being emotionally intimate, you can guarantee a relationship filled with personal growth and commitment.

Chapter Twelve | The Authentic Self

What Have I Learned From This Chapter That Applies to Me?

The Authentic Self | Chapter Twelve

What Will I Begin To Do Differently?

Chapter Thirteen
Speak My Language Too

When I was a student of psychology, I met a psychiatrist who introduced me to an interesting concept. He said more friendships and partnerships would succeed if each person learned how to speak the other's language. I didn't really understand what he meant until I started counselling, and it soon became clear.

Speaking someone's language means to know the other person well so you can communicate with them in a way they will understand. It doesn't mean using the same vocabulary. It means getting under their skin to learn how they tick. For example, are they bright-eyed and roaring to go in the morning, or do they need time to slowly wake up? Do they like to make decisions immediately, or do they like to sleep on it? Do they speak directly and frankly about issues or beat around the bush and say little? Is their communication style assertive or passive? Do they like all the details or only a few? Are there particular subjects that are taboo? How do they like to enjoy *quiet time*? Do they need help expressing their thoughts and feelings?

The list is as long as there are people. Learning these small intricacies about your friends and family is guaranteed to enrich the quality of your relationships.

I can begin by using a friend of mine as an example. When I make a decision, I mentally work through a pros and cons list, study the options, and chose what I think to be the best one. I like to work through this process in fairly short order because I like resolution. On the other hand, my friend likes to mull things over. She'll give something some thought, then leave it, and return to it later. It may take her a few weeks to make a decision depending on the issue.

For example, if I wanted to introduce an idea, like vacationing abroad together I know I would have to give her a few months' lead time. It would put her in a difficult position if I expected a response sooner.

I also tend to be fairly direct when I speak. She likes this because she always knows what I am thinking. As she says, "There is no guesswork to you." My friend on the other hand, tends to keep her thoughts and feelings to herself. She doesn't feel comfortable being direct. I know therefore, if something is on her mind, I will not try to force it out of her because it will only upset her. I need to give her time to work her thoughts through before she can venture into conversation, if ever.

I hope you are beginning to see what it means to learn how to speak the other person's language. If you have a friend or partner who is shy, withdrawn, and intimidated by crowds, you don't want to walk her into a ballroom of two hundred guests and present her with a surprise birthday party and expect her to give a speech.

🔍 The Case of Linda and Phil

Linda and Phil had been married for twenty-eight years. They had been on a trial separation for two months before seeking counselling assistance. Phil had always been self-employed in a successful construction business. Linda had been a stay-at-home mom raising their three sons, now grown. They showed a clear need to learn to speak each other's language.

Linda became incensed almost every time Phil opened his mouth. She was offended when Phil referred to her being a "housewife." She thought he was devaluing her contribution to the home. Phil, however, thought the contrary and believed he was complimenting her on her skills. She practically tore his face off when he told me her brother had suffered from alcoholism. That subject was simply taboo. When we discussed their sexuality, Linda became agitated when Phil disclosed he became quickly aroused by fondling Linda's

Chapter Thirteen | Speak My Language Too

breasts and expressed disappointment when Linda withheld that part of her body. She didn't associate that kind of foreplay with intimacy. She just wanted to be held or have her feet rubbed. Linda felt neglected by Phil because he liked to unwind by puttering around the house for a few hours on Sunday afternoon. Linda, on the other hand, had completed her weekend chores by Saturday night and was ready to go out and visit with friends and family on Sunday. And finally, Phil had difficulty verbalizing his feelings, which Linda interpreted as being robbed of his affection.

On many levels, Phil and Linda could not speak each other's language, and it took several months of therapy to begin rebuilding a language they could both speak and understand.

The Case of Mary and David

Mary came for individual counselling suffering from low self-esteem and a dismally dysfunctional marriage. She and David had been married for twelve years. She complained he never seemed to have time to talk about important matters. He was vice president of a large company and was always hopping on the company jet, participating in teleconferences or in board meetings, on the telephone with international clients, or talking to his financial advisor. She felt ignored and left out of his life. Furthermore, she was left to make decisions about their family on her own, which she found burdensome. When she would approach David to talk about these issues, he would say, "Do what you think is best." Things really came to a head when their daughter was deciding what universities to apply to, and David was too busy to provide meaningful input.

In counselling, Mary and I talked about learning to speak the other person's language. I suggested Mary begin to communicate with David via e-mail and written message. She was to become a regular contributor to his e-mail in-basket. At the same time and in recognition of his hectic schedule, when wanting a decision, Mary would present David with a series of options. By doing this, David could get a good grasp of the topic, process the information, review the options, and add his own thoughts as well. The system worked brilliantly. By doing this, their real physical time spent together became their personal quality time instead of a tug-of-war arguing about issues. Not only did Mary and David communicate more frequently, but David was also inclined to e-mail "I love you" notes.

While on the topic of e-mail, I might add, when counselling people who have recently separated, I often suggest they communicate with their ex-spouse via a written note, voice mail, or e-mail. During this time, people's feelings are hurt, their nerves are raw, and they are either seething with anger or sorrow (or both). Sometimes speaking verbally together only leads to additional upset. Communication via another medium gives the sender the opportunity to gather their thoughts, present them logically and briefly, and guarantee you won't become involved in an argument.

It takes time and patience to truly learn the meaning of speaking someone else's language. You not only have to listen with your ears but also with your heart. You need to become the pupil rather than teacher, and above all, you need to laugh along the way.

👉 Points to Remember From Chapter Thirteen

- Speaking someone else's language means to know the other person well enough to be able to communicate with them in a way *they* will understand.

- Don't assume others think the way you do. Everyone is unique.

- Don't try to force someone into a conversation they are not prepared to have.

- If someone is focused on something, it is unwise to try and bring their focus elsewhere.

- Try to stick to the facts when speaking. Dressing it up too much can lead to overload.

- If you or the person with whom you wish to communicate are emotionally charged, find a neutral form of communication, for example, e-mail.

- Practice, practice, practice.

- Keep your sense of humour.

What Have I Learned From This Chapter That Applies to Me?

Chapter Thirteen | Speak My Language Too

What Will I Begin To Do Differently?

Chapter Fourteen
Let Go, Look for the Win-Win—You Don't Have to Prove You're an Expert

Difficulties in communication often arise when one person wants control and needs to prove their idea is better than yours, or prove you are wrong or wants to become embroiled in a competition. Approaching communication with an "I'm better/smarter or more tuned in" attitude is a sure recipe for failure.

If we go back to chapter 5 and look once again at the significant people with whom Mary communicates and her corresponding feelings when with certain people, a theme arises. Mary feels less comfortable in the company of her mother, son, sister, ex-husband, boss, and night-school teacher because all display characteristic controlling behaviours. These behaviours include being judgmental, angry, snobbish, insulting, dictatorial, patronizing, and aloof. Controlling behaviours can also manifest in a much more subtle way: the person who is sweet and kind but makes you feel guilty over something you have said or done, the generous person who offers you something freely and then reminds you about it later, the person who is only trying to help you by their criticism, the person who says yes to you all the time and then goes against their word.

I'm sure you could come up with your own list easily.

Going back to this book's introduction, we learned healthy communication is based on mutual respect and positive regard. This basic and important principle leaves no room for control. Mutual respect and positive regard will result in a win-win situation for both parties even if you agree to disagree. Trying to prove you are an expert will only leave you the greater fool. Life's natural forces will eventually prove you wrong. Life is never static but ever changing. It is impossible to be an expert on everything, and besides, who would want to be?

The best way to develop positive communication is to trust and believe in the other individual. It is easier to believe than disbelieve. In other words, let the person know you trust and believe that what they think and feel is real for them. In this way, you remove all judgment. You don't necessarily have to agree with them, but in taking a non-judgmental position, you remove all attempts to control or be controlled.

If you disagree with what they are saying (even if it is against you), don't get into a debate over it. Validate and respect the other by listening. If they are presenting to you in a respectful, caring manner, listen to what is being said. If you are sincerely participating, you can continue by asking open-ended questions like, "Tell me more about that" or "I'm interested in knowing more about how you are feeling." Become the active listener, paraphrase, and check in to make sure you understand. Don't argue or become the expert. If you don't agree, don't throw stones; simply tell the person you have heard them completely and, if necessary, say you don't fully agree. This is how emotional intimacy grows. It is the ability to share potentially uncomfortable information in a threat-free environment.

The Case of Mona

I received a call from Mona requesting an appointment because she and her four siblings were being torn apart over an incident involving her youngest sister, Carol, and her parents. Carol and their two brothers were sided against the parents. Mona and her older sister were siding with the parents and by default against their other three siblings. It was a terrible mess; it affected visiting between the cousins, family dinners, and festive occasions.

This was a good time to introduce the concept of win-win. First of all, you have to make sure a problem belongs to you. In this case, the problem only belonged to her youngest sister and her parents. It did not belong to any of the remaining siblings. Once having come to this realization, Mona had to go about the business of healing the relationship between herself and her younger sister and two brothers. We looked for the win-win. Remember, you must always validate the person with whom you are communicating.

Mona and I role-played the conversation she would subsequently have with her sister and brothers. It went like this.

> MONA. Carol, I would like to do whatever I can to mend the distance between us. I feel every sad over what has happened. I think I could have done a better job at handling things.
>
> The issue between you and Mom and Dad does not involve me. Although I don't agree with your approach, I recognize it is none of my business, and it was wrong of me to take sides and judge you.
>
> What is important to me is that you and I continue to get along and our children continue to play together free of the tension which currently exists. I would like to make things better between us.

Mona's sister reluctantly agreed. However, the long-standing anger within Carol did not initially subside. Things did not improve right away, but Mona had the satisfaction of knowing she had extended the olive branch and tried to make things better.

Four months later and to Mona's surprise, she received a phone call from Carol suggesting the two of them begin counselling to repair their relationship. In counselling, we reviewed a few very important concepts. To begin and as a repeat, you must determine who owns the problem. If it does not belong to you, stay out of it! Becoming involved in another person's drama is called "triangulation," which, when acted upon, compounds pre-existing problems. So keep out of other people's business (especially family). Second, listen and speak from the heart. The goal is to develop an understanding, not to win. Next, listen and respond with, "Thank you for sharing your thoughts and feelings." Never say, "You're wrong or become argumentative!" And lastly, the goal is resolution, not to be the winner. There is no "I" in TEAM.

The win-win concept is particularly important when communicating with our children. Our job as parents is to provide our children with guidance and boundaries. It is not to run a dictatorship. This is our opportunity to teach our children the concept of win-win by example. The older our children become, the greater is our opportunity. By the time our children are in middle school, they have long known right from wrong, are learning from their mistakes, and are beginning to make decisions on their own. Create a nonthreatening, open environment to encourage your children to share their authentic selves with you. My grandmother used to say, "We only have the loan of our children. Ultimately, they must become their own person." Give them every opportunity to become a great team player.

👉 Points to Remember From Chapter Fourteen

Win-win communication means the following:

- Avoiding controlling behaviours, subtle or otherwise.

- Not judging others.

- Showing mutual respect and positive regard. Validate.

- Even if you disagree with someone, applying mutual respect and positive regard will result in a win–win for both of you.

- Trusting and believing what other people think and feel is true to them. Everyone's thoughts and feelings are 100 percent real.

- Participating actively by asking open-ended questions, paraphrasing, and checking in.

- Not acting like the expert which will result in you looking the fool.

- Believing in the other individual. It is easier to believe than disbelieve.

- Knowing when an issue/problem does and does not belong to you.

- Being prepared to agree to disagree, but remember, no one wants to lose face.

- Being an example for your children as a good team player.

Chapter Fourteen | Let Go, Look for the Win-Win—You Don't Have to Prove You're an Expert

What Have I Learned From This Chapter That Applies to Me?

What Will I Begin To Do Differently?

Chapter Fifteen
Respect Yourself, Validate Others

This chapter is being written especially for those who have recently separated. I review the concepts of respect and validation time and time again throughout therapy when seeing a client who has just left or been left by their partner.

Separation from your partner is one of life's cruelest times particularly if there are children involved. Your thoughts and emotions are a jumble of disconnected confusions. You feel as if your skin is being slowly removed, and there is nothing you can do to stop the torture. The pain doesn't seem to end. Day after day, as lack of sleep and weight loss take over, you begin to think life will never be normal again.

At this time the fight-or-flight syndrome is truly at its very best, and given there is rarely the energy, opportunity or money to take flight, the fight reaction usually comes to the fore. In the early stages of separation, this is to be expected and is normal. It is all part of the grieving process. But to carry the fight reaction on beyond its natural limits is to only harm you and those you love. No one likes to witness or participate in a confrontation. I have, all too often, seen people argue and fight with ex-spouses up to three years following the separation. To what end? Arguing is not going to return the relationship to its original healthy state. It will not improve your financial status, health, or feelings of self-worth. It will not bring Mommy or Daddy back to their children in their original capacity, and it will not guarantee your mutual friends will remain your friends. At no other time is counselling more crucial.

I have witnessed people become very ill out of anger. They start by not eating or sleeping, which upsets the chemistry of the body and debilitates the mind. Then they move on to sleeping pills or liquor or both. Then there is the constant screaming and yelling at the children and disassociation of friends and family. This is all followed by poor performance at work and, at times, loss of employment altogether. All the while they're thinking, "I'll show her [or I'll show him]. Who does she [he] think she [he] is treating me like this?" Then the downward spiral of despair begins once again.

The sadness here is that people in this condition, rarely realize what is happening to them. They fall prey to forces more powerful than their fortitude, and the snowball just grows larger and larger as it sweeps down the mountain, often taking unsuspecting victims (children included) with them. Although I was raised by a mother who believed "God helps those who help themselves," her hypothesis was repeatedly put to test over the many years I worked with those in receipt of welfare assistance. The caseload was never less than ninety families. It never changed in number during my thirteen-year employ. These cases were not comprised of ill or infirm individuals no longer able to work but were often comprised of healthy people who had given up on life and themselves. They no longer saw value, no longer believed in hope, and no longer cared. Somewhere along the way, they allowed life to swiftly and unknowingly slip beyond their grasp, leaving their heart and hands empty.

This is not to say all people who separate are going to end up dependent on drugs or alcohol and on welfare - far from it: I didn't. But I have seen enough pain and suffering in this arena to know there is no better time to introduce the concept of communicating in a way that commits to mutual respect, positive regard and validation.

When you respect yourself, you do not ignore, hurt, or abuse yourself. You do not participate in activities which will take away your spirit or the wonderful gifts and talents you have. Self-respect gives you courage, steels

Chapter Fifteen | Respect Yourself, Validate Others

you in difficult times, and allows you to understand and find compassion for the human condition. Self-respect helps you to see the light at the end of the tunnel and know most of life's challenges are transient. While counselling people who are suicidal, I always say, "You never have to choose a permanent solution for a temporary problem."

Self-respect also means not lowering yourself to someone's insults, sarcasms, or allegation of ill doing. In other words, if your ex is filling your ear with expletives, your recourse should not be to volley the same back. Appropriate action would be to either remove yourself or to say, "When you are prepared to speak to me properly, I would be pleased to hear what you have to say." Again, it comes back to being your authentic self.

Self-respect also means validating where your ex is coming from. I am not suggesting you validate the insults and sarcasms, but you can validate the feelings behind them. For example and in reflecting back to the previous example, it is useful to say, "I can understand you are very angry and upset, but until you are prepared to speak to me properly, I am not prepared to listen."

Separated couples with children are going to have to speak to one another over a myriad of topics during the course of the children's upbringing. Discussions relating to child support, visiting schedules, school, vacations, illness, pets, bedtimes, sleepovers, diet, and friends, only to name a few, will be regular topics of discussion between parents. It is useful, for the sake of the children and for your own salvation, to learn to communicate with your ex from a place of respect and validation. It is much wiser to learn this sooner than later. Habits are easily formed, and it is much better to develop a habit of positive rather than negative communication.

For people who continue having difficulty communicating following separation, I counsel them together and teach them effective communication skills. In other words, the couple takes "how to communicate with my ex" classes. How it works is quite simple. The couple continues their ongoing communication, but when they reach a volatile topic area they automatically "park it" and do not go into it further. It is better to say nothing at all if what you have to say will be nonproductive and lead to regret. The goal is to improve communication, not the reverse.

I see the couple weekly whereupon they bring a list of topics both have agreed to "park". They understand the office is the *safe place*, the place where sensitive areas of issue can be brought forward without fear of either being attacked. Remember both participants have committed to learning how to communicate better together - even if it means taking lessons. It works wonderfully.

The process is very simple. The few ground rules we abide by includes the following: no yelling, no name-calling, no butting in, no swearing, and, mutual respect and positive regard prevail. I begin by asking the couple to decide on a topic they would like to introduce first; then we begin.

The Case of Susan and Cosmo

Susan and Cosmo had been separated for two and a half months. Cosmo rented a condominium a few blocks from the marital home where Susan remained with the children - Kiley, aged five; and Tara, aged two. It was a good arrangement, as Cosmo was still able to take Kiley to school each morning, and the girls were able to sleep over at their father's home according to a prearranged visiting schedule.

The first issue to be discussed was brought forward by Susan. It concerned ensuring consistency around a bedtime routine.

Just prior to the separation, Tara had *graduated* out of her crib and into a *big girl's bed*. The difficulty was Tara's awareness of how easy it was to get out of bed any number of times throughout the night and either wake Kiley up or crawl into her parents' bed. Or, on the other hand, once put to bed, get up after bedtime kisses and demand to watch television.

Susan, a schoolteacher, claimed she had implemented some behaviour management techniques which were successful in preventing Tara's negative bedtime behaviours. Susan said her system worked fine until the children stayed with their father, whom she claimed didn't follow her system. She claimed dad let the girls "do whatever they wanted," any time of night, including staying up until 11:00 PM. They also woke up early and crawled into their dad's bed before the morning alarm sounded.

Chapter Fifteen | Respect Yourself, Validate Others

Susan noted the children returned from their dad's home tired and crabby and having forgotten the bedtime routine she had so successfully implemented. The conversation went something like this.

> SUSAN. I don't want the children sleeping at your house any more. You don't follow my bedtime routine with them; you let them run wild through the house until all hours of the night. I know because when you phoned me the other night at 9:30 PM, I could hear Tara screaming in the background. You have never disciplined the girls and leave me to deal with their crankiness upon their return, making me look like the bad guy all the time, which isn't fair. You're not fit to have them stay overnight.
>
> COSMO. You are exaggerating. You don't know what goes on in my home, and furthermore, it's none of your business.
>
> SUSAN, *now sitting upright with voice escalating*. What happens to our girls is my business, and I think you're lying. Kiley even told me Tara wakes her up during the night, and they both crawl into bed with you.
>
> COSMO. So now you're using Kiley to spy on me.
>
> SUSAN. No, I'm not. I can't prevent her from talking to me.
>
> COSMO. Yea right, and what else do you interrogate her about, my sex life?
>
> SUSAN. Don't you remember - you don't seem to know what that is!

At this point, I interjected, and we replayed the scenario with some coaching. I began by pointing out a few simple things both Susan and Cosmo had agreed to:

1. As parents, they have an obligation to make decisions based on what is fair and best for the girls. The children's ultimate well-being is the priority.

2. Susan and Cosmo both agreed to share the children between them. It was important the girls have lots of time with both parents.

3. Susan and Cosmo recognized they would have difficulty discussing some issues, therefore decided to bring those issues to my office. Congratulations for being able to park this issue until now.

4. The reason for coming to the office was to resolve issues and not make things worse.

5. Both agreed to adhere to the basic ground rules when discussing difficult issues.

I then asked Susan to present her concerns to Cosmo by using *I* words instead of *you* words, to speak from both her *thinking* and *feeling* self to validate Cosmo's position at the same time. It took a few trial runs, but the end result went like this:

> SUSAN. I know it is important for you to see the girls often and have them sleep over at your house. However, I am having a difficult time getting them back into a bedtime routine after they have stayed over at your place. I think the bedtime rules are different at your house than they are at mine. Besides, when the children return to me after being with you, they are tired and cranky. This isn't healthy. I also don't like looking like the disciplinarian all the time while I try to get them back on track. I always feel like the bad guy. Perhaps they are too young to be having sleepovers at your house.

This presentation was very good. Susan began by validating Cosmo's need to see the children often. She used lots of *I* words instead of pointing fingers at Cosmo, and instead of coming down with the ax saying she didn't want the children sleeping over at their dad's, she suggested the girls were too young. She supported her presentation by saying the children returned tired and it put her in the uncomfortable position of being the disciplinarian. She also spoke from both her *thinking* and *feeling* self.

> COSMO. I don't think the children are too young to stay overnight with me. It would break my heart if I couldn't tuck them into bed and read bedtime stories to them. You are right; I do have a hard time disciplining the girls, and I haven't really been sticking to the routine. I could use some guidance around following the schedule.

Chapter Fifteen | Respect Yourself, Validate Others

Bravo, Cosmo! By not being put on the defensive, Cosmo was able to concur with a lot of what Susan was saying. He also recognized he needed some guidance around setting boundaries, enforcing the bedtime routine, and handling Tara's middle-of-the-night wake-up calls. Eventually both Susan and Cosmo recognized it would not be fair to the girls to disallow them the opportunity to sleep at their dad's home. Both Susan and Cosmo were successful in putting their anger aside and learning to communicate from a place of mutual respect, positive regard and validation.

At this point, I talked about the importance of providing children with firm but fair guidelines, the need for consistency, and how it takes time for everyone, parents and children alike, to adapt to new ways of communicating and behaving.

Susan, still feeling somewhat reluctant and still harbouring feelings of hurt and anger over the recent separation, continued with the following:

> SUSAN. I hear what you're saying, Cosmo, but I really don't think it will work. I want some timelines built around this new approach.

I then asked Cosmo if he felt comfortable with this request and, if so, how much time he would need to master the bedtime routine. Cosmo suggested three months. Susan was adamant she would not wait longer than one month. They agreed to six weeks.

Susan and Cosmo agreed to meet following our session so Susan could review the behaviour management techniques with Cosmo so he could begin implementation. By Susan and Cosmo committing to work together, they were off to a good start. We agreed to discuss the issue together in six weeks time unless otherwise indicated.

A communications coach is invaluable at a time like this. You are able to learn new approaches to effective communication, which are transferable to a number of situations both at home and at work.

Let's take a look at another case example, which is unlike the case of Susan and Cosmo.

Respect Yourself, Validate Others | *Chapter Fifteen*

🔍 The Case of Fern and George

Fern and George were both producers of television commercials. They had been married for five years but over time had drifted apart. Much of their time was spent shooting in different international locales. They rarely saw each other. In five years both had acquired a different set of friends, different culinary inclinations, opposing vacation preferences, and so on. Fern also wanted to have a family, but George, to her surprise, had recently announced his lifestyle really didn't leave much room for a family. On top of that, Fern, while helping George pack for a business trip, found a condom in his travel kit. Fern and George had not used condoms since they were dating. When Fern questioned George, he simply shrugged and said he had just picked up the toiletries from a hotel guest basket and thrown them all into his travel kit - no big deal. Nonetheless, Fern felt uneasy.

By the time Fern and George arrived for counselling, they were both so angry they could barely stand being in the same room. They had decided on a temporary separation to give each of them time and space to think about their relationship and seek counselling.

I asked each of them, in turn, to tell me their understanding of what was going on between them. George offered to begin.

He began by essentially saying Fern had become a spoiled brat. He claimed Fern had gotten into the business easily due to his influence, and over the course of their marriage had become more demanding, possessive, and intolerant. He said Fern always wanted life to go her way and would pout for days if it did not. He regretted, in some respects, marrying someone ten years his junior but, at the time, believed she would mature. He was also disappointed that her artistic talents had not developed more than they had under his tutelage.

We were only a quarter of the way into the session, and Fern was already in tears, calling George a lying and pompous b———. Due to Fern's emotional state, she was unable to give her side of the story. That was acceptable. People have to find their own time and their own way in situations of this kind.

This was a good time for me to introduce the concept of *communications coaching*. Until Fern and George could communicate properly together, there was little use for couple counselling.

Chapter Fifteen | Respect Yourself, Validate Others

I introduced the ground rules of mutual respect, positive regard and validation. I also talked about how easy it is to blame our partner when things go wrong, but suggested our time was better spent learning more about themselves and how each had contributed to the current situation. Blame is a lousy escape route. It just doesn't work.

I asked George to begin his story again. This time, however, he was not to make any derogatory comments about Fern or point fingers and was to play by the game rules of mutual respect, positive regard and validation. With some coaching along the way, the story sounded quite different. It went like this:

> GEORGE. I met Fern while shooting on location in Paris. She was a student at the time. She reminded me of how exciting our line of work can be. She was filled with enthusiasm, and I admired how quickly she learned. I fell in love with her youthful energy and gladly took on the role of lover and mentor.
>
> We were married within six months and traveled for a month abroad following our wedding. I have always earned good money, and I loved to lavish her with an extravagant life by most standards.
>
> It didn't take Fern long to become well established in the business as well. Before we realized it, we were both off working in various parts of the world. We didn't seem to see much of each other, or I didn't make the effort. Before long, what I had originally felt toward Fern began to evaporate. All that was left were long-distance phone calls and Fern constantly pleading with me to come home or cut a job short or not take a job at all so we could be together. When we did get together, there were more pleas for dinners out, parties, vacations together, jewelry, etcetera. I felt like I was expected to be the man I was on our honeymoon forever, and for me, life is just not like that. My work is my priority, and I'm surprised Fern doesn't realize it. I feel like she hates me sometimes because of it. I feel very pressured.

Well done, George! By this time Fern had stopped crying and was listening to him intently. It almost seemed as if she was being enlightened, as though George had never said this to her before. Perhaps he hadn't.

George communicated well because he owned what he believed to have gone on in the marriage and respected himself enough to avoid falling into the ugly game of name-calling and blaming. He told his story with honesty and integrity. He validated Fern as a person and as an artist. Above all, he shared his thoughts and feelings even though what he had to say was not easy. He took the risk of changing how he communicated, and it worked.

Fern and George continued counselling for two and a half months over which time they decided on a permanent separation. The communications coaching worked admirably as they sorted out their feelings and life directions. They separated amicably, and I believe they will be able to remain friends. Due to their newly acquired communication skills, they were able to leave the relationship remembering the positives of their time together. They also recognized each played a role in the demise of their marriage and learned from that experience. Both Fern and George were able to transform their grievances into positive energy to move forward to new beginnings.

Chapter Fifteen | Respect Yourself, Validate Others

👉 Points to Remember From Chapter Fifteen

- Experiencing the fight-or-flight syndrome following an argument or upset is normal and to be expected.

- Continuing either syndrome beyond its normal limits is not healthy.

- Anger can become self-destructive. Counselling is invaluable (if not absolutely necessary) when you are faced with a major life-changing event, for example, separation or job loss.

- Self-respect prevents self-abuse and gives you courage allowing you to see the light at the end of the tunnel.

- Self-respect also means respecting others by validating them.

- It is imperative to learn to communicate with others from a place of mutual respect, positive regard and validation, especially if children are involved.

- Taking "how to communicate" lessons from a professional is a great idea. You will not only become a better communicator, but you may also develop some insight about yourself along the way.

- Learn how to park an issue until you can address it properly.

- Remember the game rules: (1) no yelling (2) no name-calling (3) no butting in (4) no swearing (5) mutual respect (6) positive regard, and (7) validation.

- Own your own thoughts and feelings, stick to the facts, and don't blame others.

Respect Yourself, Validate Others | Chapter Fifteen

👉 Points to Remember From Chapter Fifteen

- Turn negative, angry energy into positive motivation.

- If you are having suicidal thoughts, *do not choose a permanent solution to a temporary problem*. Seek counselling immediately or go to a mental health clinic or hospital.

- Life is what you make it to be. Take the opportunity to make it better!

Chapter Fifteen | Respect Yourself, Validate Others

What Have I Learned From This Chapter That Applies to Me?

Respect Yourself, Validate Others | Chapter Fifteen

What Will I Begin To Do Differently?

Chapter Sixteen
The Learning Curve

How many times have you heard or said, "You can't teach an old dog new tricks"? I must emphatically reply, "Not so, dear Watson, not so!" It is impossible to go through life without learning new things along the way. We may not always want to learn them, and the speed at which we learn may change, but Mother Nature will not allow us to stagnate. We are creatures who seek comfort and will do what is necessary to ensure it. What does this have to do with communication, you ask? In this chapter, I will show you how your communication can influence and even change the behaviour of others.

Let's begin with a simple example we learned from chapter 4. If you ignore or pay minimal attention to the inappropriate behaviour of a child but praise his/her positive behaviours, the positive behaviours will eventually prevail, and the negative behaviours will be extinguished. Engaging in prolonged communication over negative behaviour will only reinforce it. Negative reinforcement is better than no reinforcement at all and almost always guarantees the behaviour will continue.

The Learning Curve | Chapter Sixteen

A few weeks ago, I met a couple looking for some parenting suggestions. They have two children ages nine (Jasmine) and five (Blossom). Over the past four months, there have been increasing difficulties with the five-year-old who has begun having temper tantrums (at any time in any place) and refuses to follow direction. Her mother gave the following example, which involved asking Blossom to get dressed after breakfast. They were going to visit Grandma:

> MOTHER. Jasmine and Blossom, it's time to get dressed so we can go and visit Grandma. Please run upstairs and start putting your clothes on. I'll be up in a minute as soon as I put these dishes away.

Blossom's response was to stare her mother down in the kitchen and not move.

> MOTHER. Come on now, Blossom, we have to get ready. We don't want to keep Grandma waiting.

Blossom's response was to stare her mother down in the kitchen and not move.

> MOTHER. Blossom, I would like you to cooperate with me, or I'll have to pick you up, take you upstairs, and dress you myself. Please go up stairs and put your clothes on.

Blossom's response was to stare her mother down in the kitchen and not move.

Mom finally picked Blossom up and carried her to her bedroom kicking and screaming. She began undressing the child through screams of protests while battling a few kicks along the way. The behaviour continued after Blossom was dressed and carried on through the house right to the front door where Blossom then refused to put on her snow suit. A repeat of the forced dressing and screaming ensued. Blossom then had to be carried to the car and forcibly put into her car seat.

Not a very nice way to start the day for either Mom or Blossom.

The importance of any interaction is to ensure the person with whom you are communicating knows your limits and knows you mean business. No means no - not some of the time but all the time. People also have to learn they are responsible for their behaviour and there will be consequences to poor behaviour. Moreover, people also must know they do not have to put up with someone else's poor behaviour. And lastly, behaving consistently is the key to success.

In Blossom's case, we reviewed some simple guidelines, including the following:

1. Blossom should know her parents do not support poor acting-out behaviour.
2. Blossom should know what the consequence of poor behaviour will be, for example, a timeout.
3. Blossom should know what the reward of good behaviour is, for example, praise, hugs, kisses, etc.
4. Mom should not repeat her request to Blossom over and over again giving Blossom the opportunity to refuse the request to get dressed and feel empowered.
5. The more Mom talked to Blossom, the more Blossom was rewarded. Mom's attention is what Blossom wanted. Blossom's refusals compelled Mom to continue speaking to her, thus playing into Blossom's poor behaviour.

If we were to repeat the above scenario using these new guidelines, it would go something like this:

> MOTHER. Jasmine and Blossom, it's time to get dressed so we can go and visit Grandma. Please run upstairs and start putting your clothes on. I'll be up in a minute as soon as I put these dishes away.

Blossom's response was to stare her mother down in the kitchen and not move.

> MOTHER. If you don't start putting your clothes on now, Blossom, I will put you in your room for a time out until you are ready to cooperate.

Blossom's response was to stare her mother down in the kitchen and not move.

At this time, Mom would *say nothing* but approach Blossom calmly, pick her up, and take her to her room. (It is important all rooms in the home be child proof and safe.) Mom would then return to Jasmine's room and talk (in a voice Blossom could overhear) about what Jasmine wanted to wear to see Grandma, talk about any special movies or books she might like to take with her as well as what gift she could take to Grandma, etc. Mom's conversation with Jasmine would give a clear message to Blossom that only good behaviour is rewarded by Mom's attention. Mom is not going to attend to poor behaviour. Repeating appropriate timeouts consistently, not rewarding poor behaviour by extended conversation and demonstrating the rewards of good behaviour, will lead to positive change.

Both Mom and Dad practiced this new approach with noticeable improvements. It is also acceptable to have age appropriate time outs in someone else's home if the situation warrants it. Remember, consistency is the key to success.

It was also interesting to note Jasmine appeared much happier as well because Mom and Dad were not attending to Blossom all the time. Jasmine now had the shared attention of her parents.

What we have seen by this example is you can help people learn new behaviours by virtue of how you interact with them. Initially, Blossom got away with having temper tantrums and being stubborn. She was rewarded by an endless stream of conversation from her parents as they tried to persuade her into doing what they requested. All the while her poor behaviour continued because there was no consequence. Over time her behaviour eventually changed, and the temper tantrums decreased because her parents refused to reward her with their attention.

The concept of the learning curve is not just applicable to children. It is applicable to all ages. The only difference is with increased age, the person demonstrating the unwelcome behaviour will protest, more loudly, the fact that you will no longer accept their behaviour. In this case, the person's unwelcome behaviour will often escalate for a period until they finally figure out you mean business, and are totally unwilling to accept their poor behaviour.

Chapter Sixteen | The Learning Curve

🔍 The Case of Emily and Sheila

Emily and Sheila were arch rivals. At ages nineteen and seventeen, respectively, the sisters behaved like naughty children in a playground. Sheila being the younger always felt bossed about, yelled at, and put down. She did not appreciate her older sister's put-downs and insinuations, which always left Sheila feeling belittled and out of control. Given each sister had helped to program the other's "buttons", they knew how to push them whenever the occasion permitted.

One reoccurring issue was Emily offering endless negative comments about Sheila's friends. According to Emily, Sheila's friends appeared to suffer from a plethora of faults, including dumb hair, weird clothes, terrible taste in music, laziness, and on and on.

When I spoke to Sheila about this, I was interested in knowing how Sheila responded to Emily when Emily spoke about her friends like this. The normal response included Sheila going into a rampage of yelling and swearing, which sometimes ended up with articles of clothing being thrown at Emily. These outbursts would last anywhere from a few minutes to half an hour. Quite an energized communication.

After Sheila explored reasons why Emily chose to criticize her friends (poor ego strength, poor self-image, low self-esteem, jealousy, to name a few), we talked about how Sheila could communicate differently to change Emily's behaviour. I suggested Sheila begin by saying *nothing* when Emily began her oration of criticisms. That's right - absolutely nothing. The message Sheila needed to send was she was not going to play Emily's game and get caught up in her agenda. In addition, saying nothing maintains your own self-respect and dignity.

The following week I met with Sheila to hear the results of her new approach. Sheila was almost in tears. She had done exactly what I had suggested and had responded to her sister's negative comments by saying nothing. Emily became enraged and trailed around the house after Sheila, trying to goad her into responding. Sheila eventually left the house just to escape her sister's wrath. Sheila clearly thought I had given her some very bad advice. When she looked at me for guidance, I congratulated her and again suggested Sheila respond to her sister's negative behaviour by saying *nothing*. Sheila thought I had lost my mind. I explained people needed time to change and Sheila had to stay the course in order to demonstrate she was not going to participate in her sister's dialogue (game). Sheila had to be brave and believe in herself and look toward the goal of having an improved relationship with her sister.

Another week went by. Sheila's report was more promising. Emily once again became enraged when her sister did not respond to her comments, but within ten minutes or so Emily concluded her tirade by walking away while yelling, "And look at you, you're just as stupid as your friends. You can't even talk." Now, that's what I call progress. Sheila still felt a bit beat up but had to admit the argument had been less fierce than previous encounters.

Entering week three, Sheila was determined to continue with our plan, and finally - voila - success! Emily barely mentioned anything about Sheila's friends to her. In other words, Emily knew she would not get anything out of insulting Sheila for her choice of friends because Sheila wouldn't bite and participate in an argument.

Sheila told me how difficult it was for her to ignore her sister's hurtful comments and say nothing because she had to employ a *pattern interrupt* and break out of her own old patterns of behaviour (i.e., to fight back). She said she had a burning desire to scream back and counter Emily's comments with hurtful words. However, Sheila learned short-term gain (feeling better because you scream back) can result in long-term pain (a negative relationship with her sister). Sheila also discovered she was able to alter someone else's behaviour by altering her own. Yes, it was difficult at first because once Sheila changed her behaviour, Emily protested even louder because she wanted to maintain the status quo, but over time, Emily's behaviour subsided and disappeared. This is what we call the "learning curve."

Initially a change in one person's behaviour will often result in retaliation from the other person. It's important to be prepared for this and not shy away - stay the course. More often than not people will finally learn that in order to communicate with you or to have a relationship with you, their communication and behaviour have to be acceptable to you. Again, we are talking about setting your boundaries. When you set boundaries, you show people you respect yourself and thus demand their respect as well.

Diagram of Three Learning Curves

1. Current behaviour

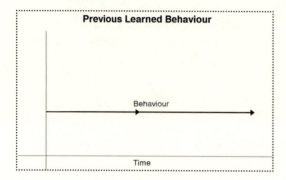

2. Newly learned behaviour and extinction back to former behaviour

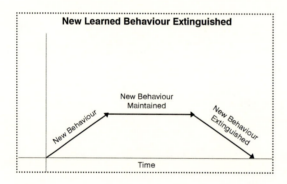

3. Newly learned behaviour and maintenance of the behaviour

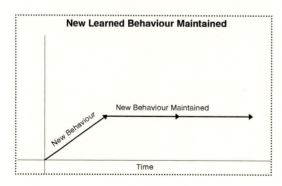

You can also apply the learning curve to yourself. For years I volunteer at a near by woman's support centre. We had a saying there. It went like this: "Fake it until you make it." This may seem funny to you, but it really does work. In other words, speak and behave *as if* you are self-confident, self-assured, and all together. If you speak and behave like that you will eventually get there. Initially you may feel foolish and self-conscious behaving in a way unlike the person you see yourself to be and you will want to stop faking it and go back to being your usual timid victim self. However, time and time again I see women emerge from their shell and blossom into strong, self confident people. Again, it goes back to getting through the initial phase of the learning curve when you feel uncomfortable. Eventually the learning curve will smooth out as you change how you choose to think, behave and communicate toward yourself and others.

Another good example involves people making lifestyle changes whether it is to stop smoking, lose a few pounds, or exercise more. Initially not having the cigarette or piece of pie or getting on the treadmill is not much fun. However, once we make it through the initial hard part, it is clear sailing. I have heard if you do anything repeatedly for twenty-one days, your mind will think you have been doing it all along. Change will come.

Now, take a few moments to reflect on your life. Are you in a relationship with someone whose behaviour you don't always appreciate, is there something about your life you would like to change, or, is there something about you personally that you would like to change? Now that you understand the *learning curve*, you can go forward and make the changes you desire. Remember, the secret to success is behaving consistently and taking baby steps. It takes nine months to make a baby for a good reason. Give yourself time to learn and change too.

Chapter Sixteen | The Learning Curve

👉 Points to Remember From Chapter Sixteen

- It is impossible to go through life without learning new things along the way.

- If you ignore or pay minimal attention to the inappropriate behaviour of a child but praise his/her positive behaviours, the positive behaviours will eventually prevail, and the negative behaviours will be extinguished.

- The concept of the learning curve is not just applicable to children. It is applicable to all ages. The only difference is with increased age, the person demonstrating the unwelcome behaviour may protest, more loudly, the fact you will no longer accept it.

- The concept of the learning curve is also applicable to yourself.

- Negative reinforcement is better than no reinforcement at all and almost always guarantees continuation of the negative behaviour. Therefore, it is not healthy to offer negative reinforcement.

- The importance of any interaction is to ensure the person with whom you are communicating knows your limits and knows you mean business. *No* means no all of the time.

- People must learn to be responsible for their behaviour, and there are consequences to poor behaviour.

- You never have to put up with anyone's poor behaviour.

- You can change or alter the behaviour of someone else by altering your own behaviour.

👉 Points to Remember From Chapter Sixteen

- It is not always easy to change your behaviour because you have to interrupt your old pattern of behaviour. In other words, you have to employ a *pattern interrupt*.

- "Fake it until you make it."

- Eventually the learning curve will smooth out as you change how you choose to think, behave and communicate with others.

- Remember, the key to success is communicating and behaving consistently and taking baby steps.

Chapter Sixteen | The Learning Curve

What Have I Learned From This Chapter That Applies to Me?

The Learning Curve | Chapter Sixteen

What Will I Begin To Do Differently?

Chapter Seventeen
Intuition

I am sitting on a beautiful sandy beach in Panama. Around me and stretching down this immense stretch of beach are a couple of hundred people, some from Canada, some from Italy, some from South America. We comprise a variety of shapes and sizes, colours, ages, and languages. Some sleep, some swim, some chat with friends and family, some make sand castles and collect shells while others sit silently and enjoy their own thoughts. What a magnificent and wonderful array of people. How different we all appear - initially.

Beyond what I can see in these people is a grand gift, which each of us posses. It's called *intuition*. Intuition - a *gut* sense you have about "something" without having the least bit of proof. A voice inside that communicates with you. The *Concise Oxford English Dictionary* defines intuition as "immediate apprehension by the mind without reasoning; immediate apprehension by a sense; immediate insight." We all have the gift of intuition, but do we all choose to listen to it? Or, are we afraid of this sixth sense or higher self or common sense? Perhaps common sense isn't that common?

In order to listen to your intuition, you must first believe in yourself. You must acknowledge there is an inner voice which is a friend living within you.

So many clients acknowledge they really knew better than to have done this or that. They knew a tiny voice within them tried to provide guidance and direction, but for a number of reasons, including lack of trust in self, insecurity, and self-doubt, they chose not to listen to their intuition, thus following the path of least resistance and eventual unhappiness.

🔍 The Case of Pam and Bob

Pam, a forty-six-year-old human resource specialist had been dating a separated man for four years. She came for counselling because of a deep sense of insecurity about their relationship. She had broken up with Bob more times than she could remember but continued to return to him.

Pam was tall with finely sculpted facial features. Her hair was chestnut brown with just the smallest amount of gray, which looked rather aristocratic. Her hair was short and stylish and showed off her slender neck, which was always adorned with a brightly coloured silk scarf, a simple gold chain, or a row of pearls.

Her long frame suited the tailored clothing style she preferred, and her loafers were of the finest leather, which always matched her handbag. At first glance nothing about this woman spoke to being *insecure*.

Pam described the on again–off again relationship she had with Bob. For long periods of time, Bob would be attentive, gentle, and loving. He would surprise her with nights out on the town, weekends at his country cottage, and gift certificates to her favourite spa. At other times, however, Bob would appear paranoid over the relationship and challenge her commitment to him. At times he would drink in excess and stalk her in her own home yelling obscenities at her. At other times he would attempt to incite an argument and, failing that, would stomp out and disappear for days. At long last, Bob would reappear as happy as a boy in springtime sporting

Chapter Seventeen | Intuition

a sensual grin, a few words of apology, a promise to change, and reservations for two at Pam's favourite restaurant. Pam always went back even though there lived a "gnawing" *sense* of discomfort within her. A sense she long ago learned to ignore.

I spoke at length with Pam about this "gnawing" or "intuitive" sense she felt yet chose to ignore. At first she said she "didn't know what it was." I believe clients *do know*; they are just too afraid to give themselves permission or credit for knowing. I rephrased the question and said to Pam, "If you did know, what would this gnawing feeling inside of you be telling you?" Pam replied by saying her intuition would be telling her to stay away from Bob, he was not to be trusted, he did not have her best interest at heart, and he was using her and punishing her for his own misdemeanors and insecurities. *Excellent, Pam!*

I asked Pam if she could truly believe in and trust her intuitive thoughts about Bob. As she looked at me, her eyes began to swell with tears, and she responded with, "I just don't know. I'd like to think I could, but I've tried so many times before and failed. I just don't know."

Pam doubted her intuitive self. She doubted the voice of reason and truth within her which if listened to, would have helped her find her way out of a very unhealthy relationship. Why? To begin, and as a review, people must believe in themselves first in order to believe their intuition is accurate. They must believe they absolutely know right from wrong, what makes them feel happy or sad, and what constitutes honourable and dishonourable behaviour. We know these things because a well-developed gut feeling
tells us so.

When you believe in your intuition you can give yourself permission to let go and not control everything. You can follow your hunches, take responsible action, and accept your lessons both good and bad without guilt or self-punishment. Intuition often paves the path of liberation. By following and listening to your intuition, you will achieve clarity of thought and peace of mind.

Let's return to the case of Pam and Bob.

Intuition | Chapter Seventeen

For four years Pam's intuition had been telling her to leave the relationship, and yet she was unable to do so. We began to examine the reasons Pam would not listen to her intuitive self. We discovered that listening to her intuitive self would mean committing to believing in herself which would mean letting go of a history of negative self-talk which had sustained her thus far. Pam's negative self talk included the following belief systems:

- I am not worth loving; I am unlovable.

- If I am not in a relationship with someone, people will think there is something wrong with me.

- I cannot and do not want to take care of myself.

- I am unable to enjoy myself if I am alone and single.

By addressing each of these belief systems, Pam was able to understand why she had never allowed herself to listen to her intuition. Subsequently, she was able to rise above her negative self-talk and trust in her better judgment. She was also able to believe she deserved to be happy and fulfilled either single or with a partner, she had a right to ask for and expect the best in life, and she could deal with challenges as they presented themselves. In other words, contentment does not come from what you have in life but how you choose to deal with life. (Are you in the driver's seat? If not, why not?)

During one of our final sessions, Pam confided that for years her intuition had told her Bob was still involved with his ex-wife. She had questioned him about this from time to time but was eager to dismiss the thought when he assured her he "hadn't spoken to her in years!" However, Pam came to believe in and trust her intuition so much she just had to test her instincts and find out for herself." She recounted the following story.

It was a warm summer evening when Bob offered to prepare Pam and her son a BBQ dinner after work. He arrived looking tanned and handsome with three large T-bone steaks, salad supplies, and some fine red wine.

Dinner was delicious. Pam and Bob enjoyed sitting on the back deck while watching the sun set. Pam had one glass of wine throughout the dinner and evening, and Bob proceeded to empty the bottle. Soon his mellow mood turned into a vicious temper. He began hurling insults at her teenage son and implied the son was involved in drugs. Pam was appalled and soon found

Chapter Seventeen | Intuition

herself in the middle of an argument between the two men. At last she called a taxi to take Bob home. She spent the rest of the evening consoling her son.

As was predictable following this kind of behaviour, Bob again disappeared for a few days. Following her intuition, Pam drove to the street on which Bob's ex-wife lived. She said she felt downright stupid sitting in her car parked several houses down from the one in which Bob's ex-wife lived. Pam's feelings of stupidity were short-lived. A car, unfamiliar to Pam, drove into the ex-wife's driveway being driven by none other than Bob. After parking the car, he and his ex-wife emerged and began unloading groceries from the car.

Pam was stunned frozen in disbelief. After listening to all of Bob's stories about how he and his ex-wife did not get along and their constant court battles, Pam could not believe her eyes. Pam sat frozen in the car, unable to move for half an hour. The only thing that shot Pam back into reality was Bob reappearing on the front lawn, preparing to cut the grass.

Pam's intuition over four long years had always been right. Inasmuch as I don't support people spying on each other, Pam did show the courage to listen to her intuition and believe in herself enough to take action and face the consequences.

Pam has never returned to that street again nor has she resumed a relationship with Bob. She is getting on with the process of grieving the relationship she chose to leave and is preparing to take on a new direction for herself and her son. Pam still has some way to go, but she now listens to the little voice within her and heeds its advice. She has made a new friend in herself and with the world at large. One can never have too many friends.

👉 Points to Remember From Chapter Seventeen

- The *Concise Oxford English Dictionary* defines *intuition* as "immediate apprehension by the mind without reasoning; immediate apprehension by a sense; immediate insight."

- Intuition is a gift each of us possesses, but only a few choose to listen to.

- Listening to and following your intuition is dependent upon a person's belief in *self*.

- To listen to and follow your intuition is to honour *self*.

- Often, and if we choose to listen, our intuition gives us our first insight that something is wrong.

- However, some people can train themselves not to listen to their intuition because they don't trust themselves enough to allow it to be their guide.

- In order to begin listening to our intuition, we have to dispose of our *negative mind tapes and negative self-talk* about self and the world.

- Listening to and following your intuition confirms you have the courage to accept and learn from the outcome.

- Listening, following, and learning from your intuition is part of the process of self-actualization.

Chapter Seventeen | Intuition

What Have I Learned From This Chapter That Applies to Me?

Intuition | Chapter Seventeen

What Will I Begin To Do Differently?

Chapter Eighteen
Determining If You Have a Disagreement

Let's start at the beginning of a "dust up" between you and someone else. The first rule of thumb is to make sure there really is a problem. So often people get into trouble because (a) they do not address the real issue at hand or (b) they think there is an issue when there is not.

Scenario A

"I was really annoyed when John kept interrupting me all afternoon while I was trying to get my work done. By the time dinner rolled around, I was ready to explode. When John brought dinner in from the BBQ that evening, I blew up at him because my steak was a little overcooked!"

Whose problem was this? Of course, it was John's wife's problem. She had an obligation to herself and to John to speak up as soon as John's interruptions began to bother her earlier in the day. It was inappropriate and unfair to her and John to not communicate with him earlier. By withholding her feelings and the truth, John's wife let her emotions and subsequent behaviour get out of hand. The lesson learned here is to not let a wound fester. Be up front and honest with people if they have annoyed, hurt, or angered you in any way. People will respect you for your openness and honesty. In addition, you are telling people you love and honour yourself and expect to be treated fairly. If you do not demonstrate and model respect for self from the outset, others will not know the boundaries within which you operate. In addition, by behaving in an up front, direct fashion, you are telling people you too prefer immediate, direct communication.

If you choose not to deal with matters directly because you fear the *assumed wrath of the other person(s)*, shame on you. No one can hurt you without your consent. Your responsibility is to take care of yourself and be honest. That means speaking up.

Scenario B

Some people believe there is discourse between themselves and another when there is not. Here, one person assumes there is an issue and responds based on their assumption, when there is no issue at all. To avoid this, you must first understand a simple fact. It is as follows: thoughts beget emotions, and emotions beget behaviour. Let's review this again. You must first have a thought before you can experience an emotion, and you must first have an emotion before you can behave.

Now that you understand this chain, let's take it another step further. Often, our first thoughts about an issue or event are incorrect even if we truly believe them to be right at that moment. So you must begin by always examining your first thought(s) before proceeding. For example, two brothers are playing on their bicycles. One brother bumps into the other brother's back tire, causing the bicycle to swerve and fall. The brother who fell can have a number of *first thoughts* which will determine his subsequent *emotions* and then his *behaviour*. The brother who was bumped could *think*, "That nasty rat, he's trying to make me fall!" In this interpretation, the following *emotion* would be anger, and the likely resulting *behaviour* would be aggression. On the other hand, let's look at an alternate first thought, "Oh no! My brother has lost his balance and is in trouble." In this interpretation, the following *emotion* would be fear, and the likely resulting *behaviour* would

Chapter Eighteen | Determining If You Have a Disagreement

be assistance. Let's try this a third time. The brother who was bumped could *think* nothing about being bumped, which would result in a neutral *emotion* and a neutral resulting *behaviour*, i.e., *life happens, no big deal*.

The rule of thumb here is to always look at your firsts thoughts to see if they are valid before you emote (have a feeling) and then behave toward someone. Amber, while in session the other day, told me of an incident between her and her husband. Husband Victor is vegan and Amber is not. Before leaving to go grocery shopping, Victor asked Amber if she would like anything specific from the grocery store. Amber asked for some yogurt. When Victor returned, he had no yogurt. Amber was upset with Victor and started an argument claiming Victor refused to bring home yogurt because it and she were not vegan. The argument ruined Amber's entire weekend.

Let's apply: thought → emotion → behaviour. Amber's first *thought* was, "Victor is mean and bigoted and will go out of his way to hurt me because I am not vegan." Amber's resulting *emotions* were hurt and anger. Amber's resulting *behaviour* was to communicate with Victor in an accusatory, aggressive fashion.

Now let's apply a different first *thought* for Amber: "Victor has a lousy memory and is too stubborn to write a grocery list before shopping." Amber's resulting *emotions* would then have been frustration and exasperation. Amber's resulting *behaviour* would have been to say, "Victor, I'd really appreciate it if we could make a shopping list together before you leave to ensure things aren't missed. I get frustrated when items we have discussed are missed." Let's do this a third and final time. Amber's first *thought* could have been, "That Victor of mine is hilarious. No matter how often I tell him what I'd like from the grocery store, I can pretty much bet he'll forget." In this case, Amber's resulting *emotion* is humour, and Amber's resulting *behaviour* is to laugh.

I am attaching this chart to assist you in examining your own *first thoughts*, *emotions*, and *behaviours* before determining whether or not you have an issue or a grievance with someone else. Let's not start something that needn't be started in the first place. Use this chart with diligence, and it will surprise you I'm sure. It is also useful in general to learn more about the way you choose to think and subsequently feel, behave and communicate.

Determining If You Have a Disagreement | Chapter Eighteen

Describe an Issue or Event

_____
_____
_____
_____
_____
_____
_____
_____
_____

My First Thoughts	Other Options for My First Thoughts
↓	↓
My Resulting Emotions	My Resulting Emotions
↓	↓
My Resulting Behaviour	My Resulting Behaviour
↓	↓

Chapter Eighteen | Determining If You Have a Disagreement

☞ Points to Remember From Chapter Eighteen

- If you think you have a disagreement with someone, make sure you are clear on what the real issue is.

- Address underlying issue(s) instead of letting your anger build and attach itself to a non-issue.

- Do not let a wound fester. Address your issue as soon as possible.

- Be honest with people. Let them know if they have upset you. Label your feeling(s) openly. Don't try to hide it. Hiding is corrosive.

- If you do not model self-respect, others will not respect you.

- If you choose to not deal with an issue because you fear assumed wrath, *shame on you!*

- You must have a thought first before you can have an emotion, and you must have an emotion before you can behave: thought → emotion → behaviour.

- Ensure your first thought is accurate before you react. Analyze your first thought and look for alternate first thoughts which could be just as feasible.

- Don't start something that needn't be started.

- Use the chart provided with diligence. It can also be applied generally to learn more about the way you think.

What Have I Learned From This Chapter That Applies to Me?

Chapter Eighteen | Determining If You Have a Disagreement

What Will I Begin To Do Differently?

Chapter Nineteen
Tools for Differing Opinions and Disagreements

I would be remiss if I neglected to talk about learning to communicate properly during a disagreement. Some of this will be a slight review of points mentioned earlier but it is well worth the review in this context. No one likes disagreements; however, it is entirely natural to find yourself in a disagreement with someone or angered by someone. Disagreements, frustration, anger, etc., are natural and healthy. In fact, when I hear people say "our marriage was made in heaven" or "we always get along" or "I live in a rainbow," I know someone in that union is not being authentic. Life is not a perfect 10. Successful people know this. A good rule of thumb is to know your marriage or partnership or friendship is normal if it is 80 percent good and 20 percent not so good.

To be realistic is to realize the rhythm of life is cobbled together with sunshine, rain, sleet and snow, heat, and cold. But, we all know when you are in the thick and chill of the most deadly winter, spring will always and predictably be just around the corner. Such is life.

The key to not just surviving but thriving during times of turbulence and discord is to know the proper rules and processes to follow. To begin, never deny your feelings. Feelings are absolutely real to us and are there to help us understand ourselves and our situation. Emotions are also the key to healing. To deny or stifle our feelings leads to internal corrosion. Honour yourself and fully experience your feelings. Also, be patient with your feelings and give them the time they need to process.

Now we know not to expect life to be a perfect 10 (remember the 80/20 rule) and we are to recognize and experience our feelings. Let's move on to how you should *approach* someone with whom you have a difference of opinion or a disagreement.

Rules to Approach

1. Don't wait too long to bring your concern or grievance to the other person's attention. People forget quickly.

2. You should say at least four to five positives to every one negative

3. Approach knowing no one is to blame. The goal is to *understand* and to *resolve*.

4. Approach knowing you are both responsible for the issue and the solution. You are equals, not opponents.

5. Remember: You can say anything to anyone in five minutes or less. Keep your delivery short and to the point. Don't exhaust the issue by continuing to speak.

6. Don't bring up the past. Be clear and current.

7. Use *I* and *me* words rather than *you*. Don't be accusatory; don't use put-downs. Come from a place of integrity.

8. Never ever, ever name-call!

9. Make sure you tell the person how you think and feel about the issue. The more you share your feelings with someone, the more emotionally intimate you become with them. In other words, you show the person you trust them enough to share your emotional self. Good relationships are built on a long history of emotional intimacy.

10. Suggest a form of resolution and tell the person what you need from them.

We can now cover what to do if someone with a concern or grievance *approaches you.*

Rules to Receive

1. Don't get uptight and defensive. The goal is always understanding and resolution.

2. Validate and respect them by listening attentively with positive regard.

3. Do not interrupt.

4. Do *not disagree* and challenge them. Your job is to **understand** what they are saying by employing active listening skills and ensuring they speak fully to the issue at hand. You must fully understand what they are telling you. (I know this is really difficult, so work at it.) Know the thoughts and feelings the person is sharing with you are real to them. You can't take that away from them.

5. Invite them to give you more information on the subject by saying things like, "Tell me more," or "Am I understanding you to say —?" or "Can you go over that point again, I don't think I understand you," etc. Show the person you want them to share with you. Invite emotional intimacy.

6. When the person has completed what they have to say, go back and tell them what you think you have just heard them say. You will be surprised how out of sync the two of you can be. It is your job to be crystal clear on what has been said to you.

7. When done listening, acknowledge you appreciate their directness and tell them you fully understand their position. Validate what they have said is important to you. You don't have to agree with it, but you must understand what they have told you, and validate them.

8. Always come from a place of positive regard, respect and validation.

After these steps have been followed, you have a few options. You can propose to reengage later after you have had an opportunity to think over what has been said. Always propose a time for re-engagement; otherwise, the person may think you are brushing their issue aside. Or, if you want to continue the conversation, you can say something like, "I think what you are saying is important, and I believe I have understood your position fully [given you have done active listening], and I would like to share my thoughts with you. Your communication might be a flat-out apology if warranted, or you may want to share your thoughts on the topic if you share a difference of opinion. At this point, you follow the same ten rules to approach set out earlier.

The two of you must continue this volleying back and forth, over and over again, each of you changing from the person who approaches to the person who is receiving until you find resolution. This may take a few minutes or a few days of engaging and reengaging. Remember, the goal is *not* to be right, but to understand what the person is saying to you and to approach the person in a way that helps them understand you. I liken this process to a game of basketball. The two of you are on the *same* team. You are *partners*. You must continue to pass the ball back and forth and back and forth up the court until the ball goes through the hoop. This work is hard! It takes discipline, diligence, and practice. No one ever got to the Olympics by jumping into the pool once.

If either one or both fall below the radar of positive regard, respect and validation, leave the conversation and commit to reconvene. When you reconvene once again, commit to following the rules as set out in this chapter.

👉 Points to Remember From Chapter Nineteen

- Disagreements are natural and healthy.

- Life is not a perfect 10.

- I believe healthy relationships are generally 80 percent good and 20 percent not so good.

- Never deny your feelings. They are real to you.

- Experiencing our emotions is a key to healing.

- You can follow specific rules when approaching someone with whom you have a disagreement. Review rules 1–10.

- Likewise, you can follow specific rules when being approached by someone who has a grievance with you. Review rules 1–8.

- Both processes require you listen with a goal to understand, not the goal of being right.

- When two people are engaged in a dispute, both parties may have to volley back and forth between the rules of approach and the rules to receive.

- It is appropriate to take a time out if necessary as long as there is a commitment to return to the subject later.

- Approach the discussion as partners on the same team, not as opponents.

- Practice, practice, practice.

- If one person becomes disrespectful, leave the conversation and commit to returning when the person regains their composure.

Chapter Nineteen | Tools for Differing Opinions and Disagreements

✏️ What Have I Learned From This Chapter That Applies to Me?

What Will I Begin To Do Differently?

Chapter Twenty
Communicating with Difficult People

Communicating with difficult people is just that - difficult! Difficult people often come from a place of aggression. They can be degrading, sarcastic, intimidating know-it-alls, bullies, and manipulators to name a few characteristics. At times like this you should be very aware of yourself so you can slow down and come from a place of calm and respond instead of react. Difficult people may employ below-the-belt tactics and attack your personhood - who you are, what you represent. I believe difficult people are defensive because they are hiding behind insecurities and a lack of self esteem. Therefore, it is imperative you do not take their attack personally. After all, whose problem is this anyway? Don't be generous enough to wear their insecurities for them.

You want to come from a place of dignity. Listen attentively to them. Employ active listening skills. Show you are *listening* to understand their point of view. Repeat back what you have heard to ensure you have understood their point. You don't have to agree with someone to listen actively. You do have to validate their point of view however. Ask for clarification or ask questions if you don't understand. Clarity is a must. By asking for clarity, you are setting the stage for fair communication. You are sending the message that what they have to say is important to you, and

Communicating with Difficult People | Chapter Twenty

you are determined to understand their position. If they are angry, let them be angry as long as their anger is not directed to you. Their emotions are real to them. Again, you don't have to own their anger. If, however, they begin to demean you, tell them you are going to leave the conversation but will return to it later when they can engage in a respectful exchange. By offering to return to the conversation, you are again sending the message you are still interested in them and what they have to say.

Use positive body language. Lean into the conversation. Be relaxed. Empathize and be genuine and smile or nod when appropriate. Show you are taking responsibility for your part of the conversation. Stay connected to the person. People are social creatures and need to feel connected to others even in times of anger.

When it is your turn to speak, choose your words carefully and stay objective. I try to speak more slowly to prevent me from blurting out something hurtful. I try to be encouraging by sending positive messages to the person. Encouragement is golden to a person who is hurting. Make sure you are being heard by the person by asking them to paraphrase what they believe they have just heard you say. People are terrible listeners especially when they are upset. People who are upset sometimes never hear what you are saying because they are so focused on themselves. You are on the same team and must keep passing the ball back and forth in a constructive way in order to get the ball through the hoop at the end of the court.

If you have to deliver a difficult message, do it with kindness. Take baby steps. People do not want to lose face. Remember to deliver more positives than negatives. No one is ever all right or all wrong. Offer to work with the person on a resolution. Ask the person what they need from you to resolve the issue. Likewise, be honest with them regarding your needs. You may have to negotiate a resolution. In the end, both parties want to be satisfied they have not had to give up all to come to a satisfactory conclusion. The resolution must be mutually agreed upon. Celebrate when resolution is achieved.

On a grander scale, you want to send the message that you are approachable. You want to send the message that should another issue arise, you are approachable and want to hear about it immediately in order to partner with them to resolve the matter. So often I see clients who have

Chapter Twenty | Communicating with Difficult People

lost the ability to communicate with their partner because their partner retaliates and attacks. Once this happens, you have destroyed all hope of positive communication and resolution.

👉 Points to Remember From Chapter Twenty

- Difficult people can demonstrate a number of undignified characteristics which is only indicative of their lack of self-esteem and insecurities.

- Do not take their attack personally.

- Do not lower yourself to their standard. Maintain your dignity.

- Listen closely to ensure you are clear as to what their issues are. Listen actively.

- If they demean you, leave the conversation and commit to returning when they are better able to behave respectfully.

- Use positive body language, empathize, and be genuine. Stay connected.

- When you speak, choose your words carefully, speak slowly, sound encouraging, and make sure the person fully understands your position. Ask them to recap what you have said. Clarify if their understanding is incorrect.

- Deliver difficult messages with kindness.

- Partner together to find resolution. No one is ever all right or all wrong.

- The resolution must be mutually agreed upon.

- Celebrate when resolution is achieved.

Chapter Twenty | Communicating with Difficult People

What Have I Learned From This Chapter That Applies to Me?

What Will I Begin To Do Differently?

Chapter Twenty-One
Forgiveness

The *Concise Oxford English Dictionary* definition of the word *forgive* includes the following: remit, let off, cease to resent, and pardon. The definition of the word *forgiveness* is the act of forgiving or state of being forgiven. I believe the word *forgive* means to "release myself" from feeling victimized, unhappy, angry, hurt, belittled, tormented, anxious, frustrated, resented, distressed, abandoned, and irritated as a result of someone's unpleasant actions or words toward me. It has very little to do with pardoning someone else's poor behaviour. I choose not to condone the poor behaviour of others. Forgiveness is an attitude, a state of mind which says I choose not to set myself up to be hurt or put down; therefore, I will forgive the person and trust and believe they will find the courage to change their ways. I am also free to have a communication with them or remove myself from an unhealthy situation.

Forgiveness | Chapter Twenty-One

🔍 Patty's Story

For years following my separation, I [Patty] really believed I hated my ex-husband. I could run miles of film through my mind reinforcing all the reasons I should hate him. I remember a time when I was actually physically ill because of anger. I lost twenty pounds, barely slept, and tormented myself with guilt and negative self-talk. Finally, the time came when I had to make a decision between living a life of agony or finding peace of mind and freedom. I chose peace of mind and freedom, freedom from beating myself up, freedom from being the poor victim, freedom from being stagnant, and freedom from living and breathing anger. I needed to give up inhaling noxious recycled old fumes and step outside to smell fresh air and see things from a different perspective. I told myself it was *time to heal*. It was time for me to examine and heal the underlying feelings which lay beneath my inability to forgive. I was willing to look beyond my ex-husband and examine myself by not rejecting my feelings.

When I looked closely at where the hate came from, I discovered it came from feelings of fear of being alone, anger from being deserted, fear of poverty, fear of being a single mom, guilt from having contributed to breaking up our family, shame for not being the wife my parents expected me to be, embarrassment in the face of family and friends, fear around entering a single's life after a decade of marriage, confusion about how to afford quality day care, and unrest about who I was as a person if I could no longer be defined as someone's *wife*.

Step number one of addressing these feelings was to stop beating myself up and remove the *expectations* I placed on myself. When I looked in the mirror, I had to begin seeing someone who was bright and loving, whose heart came from a good place, and someone who intended to do good, not evil. Someone who had valuable and unique qualities no other person could call their own.

Step number two was to question the validity of the feelings and separate what was valid from what was not. For example, when I questioned the validity of fear of being alone, I had to admit I was not alone. That fear was unfounded. I had two beautiful children; I had family who cared about me and many marvelous friends. Being separated did not leave me *alone*.

When I questioned my anger over feelings of being deserted, I decided that feeling was only half real. I had to accept responsibility for participating in

Chapter Twenty-One | Forgiveness

the ending of the marriage, but given I was now a single parent, I did still feel deserted.

When I checked my financial records and questioned my fear of poverty, I decided it was definitely a valid fear.

When I questioned my fear of being a single mom, I decided it was only a half fear. I had always done my best to be a good mom, and there wasn't any reason why I should change.

When I examined my shame for not being the wife my parents expected me to be, I decided it was pure nonsense. I only had to live up to my own expectations of self. I did not have to live up to my parents' expectations.

When I examined my feelings of embarrassment in the face of family and friends, I decided I could not waste valuable energy on being embarrassed. Energy is too valuable a commodity to waste.

When I examined my fear of being single again, I decided it was a valid fear. I couldn't imagine going on a date with a purse full of Arrowroot cookies and disposable diapers to say nothing about how to address the *sex* part.

When I examined my fear about being able to afford quality day care, I decided I could receive counsel from a local social service agency, research day care providers, and work something out.

When I examined my unrest about who I was as a person now I was separated, I decided it was a real fear but also knew I was being given an opportunity to discover myself all over again.

This examination told me a number of my feelings were not valid at all. The most valid feelings included anger, desertion, fear, and confusion.

Step number three for Patty was to begin the journey of forgiveness and *making friends with her devils*. Yes, that's right, *making friends with her devils* - anger, desertion, fear, and confusion. The counselling process helped Patty with this.

"Making friends with your devils" is a phrase I coined years ago. I believe everyone has hidden feelings which can haunt them. The way we release ourselves from being the haunted is to acknowledge those feelings or *our devils*, accept and befriend them.

Forgiveness | Chapter Twenty-One

Exercise

Give your feeling (fear, anger, frustration, etc.) a name and face. Really feel it! Experience it! Envision what it looks like in front of you. See it as a shape and in colour. In other words, make your feeling real and in the present.

Once you can see your feeling in your mind, envision taking out a gift box and some stunning wrapping paper. See yourself putting your feeling inside the gift box. Wrap the box in the paper and tie the most splendid bow on top. Admire its beauty. It is a beautiful gift box holding a piece of beautiful you.

Now, envision putting the box on the top shelf of your closet. Don't close the door. You want to be able to walk past the door, look up and say, "There sits a part of my beautiful self which no longer lives inside of me. It now lives up there and apart from me"

If and when, from time to time, your feeling jumps down and creeps back into your mind, just gently acknowledge its presence, envision picking the box up, and putting it back up on the shelf. Do this visioning exercise over and over again until you can successfully remove your feeling and put it in a *safe place*.

Another way of understanding and releasing your feelings and finding forgiveness is to journal. Journaling takes your thoughts and feelings from your mind, down your arm and out onto a piece of paper. It makes our thoughts and feelings real because you see them in writing. You don't have to write pages and pages of material, but it is important you write every day - even if it is only a few lines. Every so often review your journal and reread what you have written. You will discover things about yourself you never knew before.

I also suggest clients engage in a daily program of deep relaxation breathing. With each breath, breathe in love, courage, positive self-regard, honour, determination, and tenacity. With each breath out, exhale fear, anger, hate,

Chapter Twenty-One | Forgiveness

and negative self-regard. Put aside special time each day to do your deep breathing exercises and remember to listen to the sound of your breath. Focus your mind on breathing in positive and breathing out negative.

When I was a little girl, my grandmother taught the greatest way to forgive was to find goodness in others. To see beyond the bad to the good and live knowing goodness does exist, ro matter how great or small. I can remember returning from school one afternoon and telling Nana about a classmate who had angered me. I stomped and chattered with great aplomb. At the end of the tirade, she told me the following story. It went like this:

> Once upon a time there lived a small group of people living in a pretty rural village far away. They were farmers. They were a kind group of people who laboured working the land; raising herds of sheep, cows, and goats, and flocks of chickens. One evening a wild dog snuck into a farmer's field under the light of the moon. He was starving and killed a sheep for his dinner. The next day the farmer was furious. Each night for the next three nights the wild dog crept into other farmer's fields to hunt for dinner.
>
> Finally, the farmers called a town meeting to discuss what to do about the wild dog. They decided to gather the community together, hunt the dog down, and kill it.
>
> The next night, the community gathered after dark wearing their dark clothes and carrying their weapons. They took off in different directions to circle the farms and close in on the dog. At last the dog was spotted making his way to yet another farmer's field. The community members closed in. When they got close enough, they began to hit the dog with stones. The dog cried out in pain. Moments later, Jesus arrived and parted the crowd as he walked toward the dog that was by now lying on its back and bleeding. Silence overcame the crowd as Jesus approached the dog and knelt down beside it. At last, one voice spoke up and said to Jesus, "The dog is a killer dog; it kills our animals and eats them for dinner. The dog is old and ugly, its hair is dirty and matted, and it smells."

Soon more members of the crowd began to join in and yell out their dislike of the dog and echo the thoughts of the first farmer. It became a deafening roar.

Jesus turned and looked into the crowd. He raised his hand to silence them. He met every pair of eyes with his own and said, "But look at what beautiful teeth he has."

Initially I couldn't figure out what my grandmother was getting at, but it soon became clear that she was asking me to look for the good in the student who had so disturbed me earlier. She wasn't asking me to condone the behaviour of the student but was asking me to look beyond it. I hope you will remember this story and let it be your guide as it has been mine.

Nothing in life is simple, including forgiveness. Give yourself the time you need to go through the process. You have to be an active participant, which requires strength, honesty, and patience. It's okay to feel hurt and anger. It's important to honour yourself enough to forge forward. Feel free to seek the assistance of a therapist to help you along your way. Knowing when to get support is smart.

And remember, forgiveness is closely tied to self-respect, unconditional love, and positive regard. If you respect yourself, you will not put yourself in a place that hurts. If you love unconditionally, forgiveness will come easily. If you have positive regard for self and others, it will be very difficult to find fault.

Lose Your Expectations

The word *expectation* has been mentioned briefly. Let's take a closer look at what it means. Freeing yourself of expectations means you no longer expect your ex-husband to treat you like a friend, your boss to be Ms. Wonderful, your children to behave like angels, your parents to be perfect, your siblings be close and loving, and your friends to bend over backward, and so on. Keeping unrealistic expectation of others often leads to not having our needs met. This, in turn, only fuels preexisting feelings of hurt, anguish, anger, resentment, and bitterness. A friend of mine once said, "People continue to look for meaning and certainty in a world that offers neither."

Chapter Twenty-One | Forgiveness

Again I will remind you forgiveness and freeing yourself of expectations does not mean you condone the behaviour of others, nor does it mean you hide your opinions if someone is being offensive or hurtful toward you. Knowing what you will and will not put up with is healthy. It's called knowing your own boundaries and exercising freedom of choice. Freedom of choice means the ability to look at someone objectively, thus insulating yourself from the emotional entanglement. Freedom of choice means letting go of the struggle, redefining your relationship with another, and having the ability to change negative energy into positive attitudes and actions. Perhaps now is your time to choose to communicate with yourself differently and celebrate the coming of inner peace.

Forgiveness | Chapter Twenty-One

👉 Points to Remember From Chapter Twenty-One

- Forgiveness has nothing to do with pardoning another person's behaviour. Forgiveness means releasing yourself from the irritation someone has caused you.

- Forgiveness is a choice. The deliberate choice to release yourself from inner turmoil.

- Forgiveness releases the mind to move onto a healthier and more peaceful state.

- Choosing to forgive means choosing to heal. It means choosing to look at all sides of the story (including the part you played) and from that prism of awareness move forward to a place where you can own your own feelings and feel at rest with yourself and the other person(s).

- Owning our feelings means being able to do a reality check on what you believe and challenge old mental tapes, negative self-talk, and expectations.

- Doing a reality check on your feelings means being able to separate what is valid from what is not.

- In order to move forward, it's important to make friends with your devils - those feelings which haunt you. Recognize they are part of the beautiful you but put them into a place over which you have control so as not to allow them to control you.

- Visioning exercises are a good way to befriend your devils. Practice, practice, practice!

- Journaling is also a good way to both befriend your devils and get to know yourself better. Journaling is a healthy release.

Chapter Twenty-One | Forgiveness

👉 Points to Remember From Chapter Twenty-One

- Relaxation breathing is yet another way to breathe in positive thoughts and exhale negative thoughts.

- Look to your elders to learn more about the concept of forgiveness.

- Free yourself from expectations, expectations you have of yourself and others. Keeping unrealistic expectations about others often leads to you not having your needs met.

- Forgiveness means freedom of choice - letting go of the struggle - having the ability to change negative energy into positive attitudes and actions.

- Forgiveness does not mean condoning the actions of others.

Forgiveness | Chapter Twenty-One

What Have I Learned From This Chapter That Applies to Me?

Chapter Twenty-One | Forgiveness

✎ What Will I Begin To Do Differently?

Chapter Twenty-Two
You Will Achieve What You Believe *or* Fake It Till You Make It!

In conclusion, I would like to speak briefly on intention and how I envision our brains working. You will achieve what you believe so why not believe something better? I believe your brain is like a lake with thousands of rivers and tributaries running out and away from it. These rivers and tributaries are torrents of messages traveling out to the rest of our body. The path this waterway follows does so through habit, always searching for the path of least resistance eventually cutting an ingrained pathway into our brain. It is possible, however, to change the direction and flow of these rivers and tributaries of energy by consciously changing your thought processes and diverting the direction of previously followed paths.

If we look back on previous chapters, we learned each of us has the power and capacity to achieve what we believe by finding security within ourselves. When we feel secure in ourselves we make adult, responsible decisions and participate in life through cooperation and reaching out to others. These actions force us to expand ourselves. We are forced to learn how to communicate and cooperate with others and become a good team player. We constantly *will* ourselves to live in a win-win world where we become part of a larger whole and not the whole itself. We are able to expand and contract ourselves like an elastic band comfortably between interdependence and being with ourselves.

Chapter Twenty-Two | You Will Achieve What You Believe or Fake It Till You Make It!

When you have mastered this skill of connection, there is no need to feel inadequate because you have proven to yourself you are capable of depending on yourself and participating with others in a cooperative, caring, and sensitive way. You present yourself as a competent, reliable individual who is comfortable in their own skin and has no reason to try and control or manipulate others. You are a walking testament that you value both yourself and others and are willing to give and receive graciously. You celebrate success instead of trying to hurt others or demean them in an effort to make yourself feel better. Again, you act like an adult.

In addition, you must believe you are resilient and have the courage to face challenges and remain confident. You must never let yourself feel defeated and hopeless. The goal is to remain willing to try, over and over again, by learning and developing new skills and strategies to avoid repeating unsuccessful old outcomes. Remember, attitude equals altitude. Positive must outweigh negative; in other words, no Eeyore effect.

From the book *The Te of Piglet* by Benjamin Hoff we read the Eeyore effect.

> "What's the matter, Piglet?" asked Winnie the Pooh.
>
> "I was walking through the flowers just now," he said (Piglet), "singing a little song when Eeyore came up."
>
> "Oh. Eeyore. What happened?"
>
> "He said, 'Be careful, little Piglet - someone might pick you along with those pansies and put you in a vase on the mantelpiece. And *then* what would you do?' Then he walked away, chuckling to himself."
>
> "Oh, don't mind Eeyore. He just likes to make others feel small, especially if they're smaller than he is, anyway. That makes him look big - he thinks."
>
> "I wouldn't mind his being miserable by himself, if he enjoys it so. But why does he have to spread it around?"
>
> "There is something in each of us that wants us to be unhappy. It creates in our imaginations problems that don't yet exist - quite often causing them to come true. It exaggerates problems that are

already there. It reinforces low self-esteem and lack of respect for others. It destroys pride in workmanship, order, and cleanliness. It turns meetings into confrontation, expectations into dread, opportunities into danger, stepping stones into stumbling blocks. It can be seen at work in grimaces and frowns, which pull the muscles of the face forward and down, speeding the aging process. It contaminates the mind behind the face with its negative energy and spreads outward, like a disease. And then it comes back, projected and reflected by other unhappy minds and faces. And on it goes."

Lesson learned? No Eeyore effect!

In addition to being mindful of the Eeyore effect, we must also be aware of how our minds can trick us into having distorted negative beliefs. In this case, we do achieve what we believe, but what we believe is actually erroneous and invalid. I have worked with numerous clients whose thoughts have demonstrated a whole assortment of distorted thinking. Subsequently, they do achieve what they believe, but their belief system is faulty and distorted, leaving them the helpless victim. Examples of distorted thinking include the following:

- *The all-or-nothing dude.* "No, if you are not going to play the game my way, I am not going to play at all!"

- *The poor-me dude.* "This always happens to me!"

- *The negative dude.* "I have always been the bad apple in our family. Nothing ever goes right for me."

- *The self-loathing dude.* "I hear your compliment, but I really didn't do anything at all."

- *The self-sabotaging dude.* "Yes, I received your invitation, but I didn't respond because I thought you were just being polite. Surely you didn't want me to attend!"

- *The mind-reader dude.* "I didn't bring my grievance to your attention because I knew exactly how you'd respond, and I didn't want to go through that again."

- *The exaggerator dude.* "I'm so stupid. How could I have forgotten to bring my homework!"

- *The emotional dude.* "He must have talked behind my back. I hate him!"

- *The should dude.* "I ought to / I must / I should / I have to do this!"

- *The name-calling dude.* "You imbecile!"

- *The blame dude.* "I am late arriving because I'm not very good at managing my time."

Do you see yourself anywhere on this list? If you do, be aware that you will achieve what you believe unless you begin to change your thinking into something which is clear, realistic, precise, and true. Lesson learned? Boot the distortions dude, and communicate with yourself differently!

Another important concept involved in *achieving what you believe* is being aware of how you perceive each current moment or your current *now*. Is your perception that you are competent and capable of dealing with a challenge that has presented itself, or is your perception you are a victim of someone else's behaviour? Only when you choose to be responsible for your outcomes will you be entitled to take responsibility for your successes and failures. Believe your outcomes are achievable and define those outcomes/successes in everyday, simple language so you can understand and own them. For example, some achievable outcomes could be the following:

- I will attend school every day.

- I will take driving lessons and be successful in passing my driving test.

- I will phone my elderly aunt once a week to stay connected to her.

- I will do a better job of listening actively to my partner to show respect and commitment.

- I will adopt a healthier lifestyle. I will join the gym this week and begin making better food choices.

Be your own best cheerleader. Keep goals simple and achievable. Be realistic and make sure you do a weekly review of your successes.

In addition to taking responsibility for yourself, it's important to develop your own personal support team around you. It can be made up anyone who shares your values and goals and wants you to succeed. Sometimes we need others there to root for us when we think or feel we are unable to help ourselves fully. Know these loving people will always be there for you whether you succeed or not. The job of your support team is to do just that - support. It is not to judge.

By example, I found myself almost catatonic for several weeks, if not months, following my ex-husband's announcing he was leaving me. A doctor diagnosed me as suffering from extreme shock and trauma. I couldn't eat, sleep, or think. I just remember feeling a severe pain as if a scorching saber had cut my body in two, and the two pieces were falling separately downward and in slow motion into infinity. This intense feeling of falling was relentless.

However, rising as if out of nowhere came my sister, daughters, friends, mother-in-law, my daughter's friends, colleagues, and even some of my ex-husband's friends to not only help me but to cheer/drag/push me forward. They sent me resounding, loving messages of support and encouragement. They believed in me unconditionally. There wasn't one minute of one day that went by where I did not have a team of cheerleaders around me, believing I could achieve a full recovery. As my daughters said to me, even while shouldering their own grief, "Mom, we know you can get through this. We are your biggest fans and every day know we are waiting here at the finish line with arms open, waiting to celebrate your crossing."

Later, when I recovered, I realized, unknown to me at the time, I had spent years building a support team of cheerleaders by living my faith and instilling in them my belief in their ability to achieve what they believed. In turn, my love and belief in them came back to me when I needed strength. In my private practice, I have witnessed this same loving encouragement save lives. You too can build your team.

When you are achieving what you believe, you will feel great—on top of the world - *the best*! So how do you maintain and sustain this empowering sense of well-being and greatness all the time, when you are temporarily not believing or achieving? This is the simplest answer of all: we maintain and sustain this sense of well being through *gratitude*, by giving

Chapter Twenty-Two | You Will Achieve What You Believe *or* Fake It Till You Make It!

thanks each and every day and by demonstrating our gratitude. If I came home from school pouting or in a bad mood, my grandmother would tell me to go and do something nice for someone else. It always worked. The ability to show gratitude, thankfulness, and appreciation prohibits concentration and consumption with the self and manifests itself in something larger and apart from self. Therefore, if you believe in the strength and power of gratitude, you will achieve that same strength and power within.

Points to Remember From Chapter Twenty-Two

- "Fake it until you make it" if you have to.

- Work to consciously change your old ways of thinking. Your previous ways always looked for the path of least resistance. Now is the time for change.

- You can achieve what you believe if you first believe in yourself. Your security begins there. Only then will you be able to make adult, responsible decisions.

- When in your adult ego state, you will be able to reach out and make healthy attachments with others and create a win-win world for yourself.

- Once you have mastered this art of connection, you will show yourself as a cooperative, caring, competent, and sensitive person presenting the "achieve what you believe" philosophy.

- Resiliency will replace hopelessness, and you will develop new strategies to ensure different positive outcomes.

- No Eeyore effect!

- Delete distorted and negative beliefs.

- Be aware of how you perceive every current moment. Are your perceptions coming through a positive or negative lens? Do you perceive yourself as competent or inept?

- Define your goals/outcomes/successes in everyday language, keep them simple, and believe they are achievable. Do a weekly review.

- Be your own best cheerleader and build a support team around you.

- Give thanks and demonstrate your gratitude every day!

Chapter Twenty-Two | You Will Achieve What You Believe *or* Fake It Till You Make It!

What Have I Learned From This Chapter That Applies to Me?

What Will I Begin To Do Differently?

To all those who have taken the time to read, ponder, and hopefully learn a few things from this small book, I graciously thank you!

Patrice

Biography

Patrice has an M.S. Ed. in counseling from Niagara University. She began a social work career in 1974 at a Group Home for youth. It was a tiny residence full of filthy, worn furniture and the foul smell of must. The first day she reported for work frisky and filled with confidence. No one answered the door. When finding the door open, she entered and followed a trail of blood to the girls' bathroom. A beautiful young girl with long amber braids had just slit her wrists. Working with disenfranchised youth cemented Patrice's commitment to help others learn how to help themselves.

A year later Patrice accepted a position with regional social services where she specialized in psychiatry, mainly working with patients impacted by schizophrenia and/or bipolar illness. She was fortunate to be part of an interdisciplinary team whose responsibility it was to develop a community-based rehabilitation outreach program following the close of a nearby major psychiatric facility. The team wrote several successful community-based rehabilitation outreach programs. Moving from a client group of marginalized youth to the psychiatric population was a large and rewarding learning curve for her, to say nothing of collecting a library of memories.

After finding herself a single parent of two beautiful daughters, aged one and a half and four years, she enrolled in a graduate program and completed the degree in two and a half years - part of it while working full-time and attending school full-time, at the same time.

With an M.S.Ed. in counselling, Patrice secured a position coordinating and then managing the Ontario government's Employee Assistance Program. She sat on Niagara University's Graduate Education Council part time to prepare the University for Accreditation and further develop the graduate degree counselling and mental health programs, became a part time adjunct faculty member, and served as a part time practicum supervisor for Michigan State University's master's of rehabilitation counselling program.

While employed by the Ontario government she began a home-based counselling practice. Actually, a physician who was familiar with Patrice's expertise started the practice by divulging her phone number to a distraught patient. That was the birth of a twenty-plus-year practice.

Throughout those twenty-plus years, Patrice has volunteered at the Canadian Mental Health Association, the Women's Information and Support Centre of Halton and school boards providing workshops and seminars on communications skills, building your self-esteem, and living life holistically. She also returned to school part time to become a certified Natural Health Care Practitioner (CNHP) in order to incorporate natural health-care modalities into the therapeutic process.

She is a member of the Ontario Association of Consultants, Counsellors, Psychotherapists and Psychometrists (OACCP), Dr. Dan Dalton and Associates, and the Wellness Counselling Group. More recently, she taught for Humber College Institute of Technology and Advanced Learning in Toronto, Ontario.

It's been over thirty years since Patrice walked into that smelly group home. Her personal and professional development has been the great adventure.